M000314346

FUTILITY CLOSET 2

FUTILITY CLOSET 2

A Second Trove of Intriguing Tidbits

by GREG ROSS

FUTILITY CLOSET BOOKS

Raleigh, North Carolina

FUTILITY CLOSET 2
Copyright © 2015 by Gregory Ross

Printed in the United States of America

ISBN: 978-0-9898871-2-0

Book design by Greg Mortimer

Library of Congress Control Number: 2014913954

Library of Congress subject headings:

Handbooks, vade-mecums, etc.
Intellectual life —Miscellanea.
Amusements.
Curiosities and wonders.
Learning and scholarship —Miscellanea.
Puzzles.

www.futilitycloset.com

CONTENTS

PREFACE

Here's another collection of oddities from Futility Closet, the online catalog of captivating curiosities. It's been a busy year—in the twelve months since we released our first book, *Futility Closet: An Idler's Miscellany of Compendious Amusements*, we've received millions of new visitors to the website, and we've now launched a podcast on the Boing Boing network, which is amusing an ever-greater audience with true tales of monkey signalmen, balloon-borne sheepdogs, desert pianos, and parachuting chocolate bars.

I don't know where all this is heading, but I'm grateful every day for the opportunity to offer it to such a smart, hilarious, thoughtful audience. I'll keep ransacking libraries, but if you come across an interesting tidbit that you think our readers would like, please send it to me at greg@futilitycloset.com—we're always glad to receive new submissions. Thanks for reading!

Raleigh
April 2014

PART ONE

ROBERT BROWNING, YANKEE STADIUM, *and* HALLEY'S COMET

BOOMERANG

In seeking a costume for the character Professor Marvel in *The Wizard of Oz*, the MGM wardrobe department found a tattered Prince Albert coat in a secondhand store in Los Angeles.

One afternoon actor Frank Morgan turned out the coat's pocket and discovered the name "L. Frank Baum." By a bizarre coincidence, they had chosen a coat once owned by the author of *The Wonderful Wizard of Oz*.

This sounds dubious, I know, but cinematographer Hal Rosson, his niece Helene Bowman, and unit publicist Mary Mayer have all vouched for the story.

"We wired the tailor in Chicago and sent pictures," Mayer told Aljean Harmetz for the book *The Making of The Wizard of Oz*. "And the tailor sent back a notarized letter saying that the coat had been made for Frank Baum. Baum's widow identified the coat, too, and after the picture was finished we presented it to her. But I could never get anyone to believe the story."

● ● ●

LONG WAY HOME

In 1505 Ferdinand Magellan sailed east to Malaysia, where he acquired a slave named Enrique who accompanied him on his subsequent westward circumnavigation of the globe. When that expedition reached the Philippines, Enrique escaped, and his fate is lost to history. That's intriguing: If he managed to travel the few hundred remaining miles to his homeland, then he was the first person in history to circumnavigate the earth.

• • •

THE VALUE OF TARDINESS

One day in 1939, Berkeley doctoral candidate George Dantzig arrived late for a statistics class taught by Jerzy Neyman. He copied down the two problems on the blackboard and turned them in a few days later, apologizing for the delay—he'd found them unusually difficult. Distracted, Neyman told him to leave his homework on the desk.

On a Sunday morning six weeks later, Neyman banged on Dantzig's door. The problems that Dantzig had assumed were homework were actually unproved statistical theorems that Neyman had been discussing with the class—and Dantzig had proved both of them. Both were eventually published, with Dantzig as coauthor.

"When I began to worry about a thesis topic," he recalled later, "Neyman just shrugged and told me to wrap the two problems in a binder and he would accept them as my thesis."

• • •

CAUGHT!

When Eisenhower took office in 1953, a group of conservative Republicans claimed that the outgoing Democrats had been stealing gold deposits from Fort Knox.

Bowing to pressure from the Daughters of the American

Revolution, Eisenhower had the gold counted. Sure enough, it came up ten bucks short: The depository contained only $30,442,415,581.70.

Truman's treasurer, Georgia Clark, rolled her eyes and sent a check to cover the shortfall.

• • •

CHINESE DIET

WON TON spelled backward is NOT NOW.

• • •

THE WILLOW CATHEDRAL

For a 1793 treatise on the principles of Gothic architecture, Scottish architect Sir James Hall built an example using natural materials:

❝The wicker structure, as shewn in the frontispiece, was formed according to the plan of the cloister of Westminster Abbey, by a set of posts of ash about three inches in diameter thrust into the ground, with a set of willow rods of about an inch in diameter applied to them, the whole being conducted as already fully described. The construction answers perfectly well in practice, and affords a firm support for the thatch.

"The summit of the roof within is about eight feet high," he added, "so that a person can walk under it with ease."

• • •

BURNING TIME

You have two one-hour fuses: If you light one, it will be consumed in exactly one hour.

Unfortunately, they're badly made—some sections of each fuse burn faster than others. You know only that each full fuse will burn in one hour.

Using only these two fuses (and matches to light them), how can you tell when 45 minutes have passed?

(See Answers and Solutions)

• • •

THE PIED PIPER OF SAIPAN

Marine private Guy Gabaldon was 18 years old when he took part in the invasion of Saipan in the Mariana Islands in June 1944. In order to secure the island, Gabaldon began to go on "lone wolf" missions, using his smattering of Japanese to convince enemy civilians and troops to give themselves up.

"Immediately after landing on Saipan I decided that I would go off into enemy territory to fight the war as I saw fit," he wrote in his 1990 memoir *Saipan: Suicide Island*. "I always worked alone, usually at night in the bush. I must have seen too many John Wayne movies, because what I was doing was suicidal."

"My plan, as impossible as it seemed, was to get near a Japanese emplacement, bunker or cave, and tell them that I had a bunch of marines with me and we were ready to kill them if they did not surrender. I promised that they would be treated with dignity, and that we would make sure that they were taken back to Japan after the war."

He must have been stupendously persuasive, because he captured 1,500 Japanese single-handed—including 800 on a single day in July. "When I began taking prisoners it became an addiction," he wrote. "I found that I couldn't stop—I was hooked."

Gabaldon earned a Navy Cross for his efforts, and Jeffrey Hunter played him in the 1960 film *Hell to Eternity*. "The heroes are still over there," he told the *Chicago Tribune* at the film's opening. "Those who gave their all are the heroes."

• • •

NO ANSWER

Helen Fouché Gaines' 1956 textbook *Cryptanalysis: A Study of Ciphers and Their Solution* concludes with a cipher that, she says, "nobody has ever been able to decrypt":

VQBUP PVSPG GFPNU EDOKD XHEWT IYCLK XRZAP
VUFSA WEMUX GPNIV QJMNJ JNIZY KBPNF RRHTB
WWNUQ JAJGJ FHADQ LQMFL XRGGW UGWVZ GKFBC
MPXKE KQCQQ LBODO QJVEL.

It was still unsolved in 1968, when Dmitri Borgmann, editor of the *Journal of Recreational Linguistics*, urged his readers to tackle the problem: "Are you going to let this challenge lie there, taunting you for the rest of your lives? Or are you going to get busy and solve that pesky little crypt?"

So far as I can tell, they let it lie there, and it remains unsolved to this day. There are few clues in Gaines' book. The cipher is the last in a series of exercises at the end of a chapter titled "Investigating the Unknown Cipher," and she gives no hint as to its source. Of the exercises, she writes, "There is none in which the system may not be learned through analysis, unless perhaps the final unnumbered cryptogram." The solution says simply "Unsolved."

· · ·

THE CONSCIENCE FUND

During the Civil War, the U.S. Treasury received a check for $1,500 from a private citizen who said he had misappropriated government funds while serving as a quartermaster in the Army. He said he felt guilty.

"Suppose we call this a contribution to the conscience fund and get it announced in the newspapers," suggested Treasury Secretary Francis Spinner. "Perhaps we will get some more."

Ever since, then the Treasury has maintained a "conscience fund" to which guilt-ridden citizens can contribute. In its first 20 years, the fund received $250,000; by 1987 it had taken in more than $5.7 million. One Massachusetts man contributed 9 cents for using a damaged stamp on a letter, but in 1950 a single individual sent $139,000.

In order to encourage citizens to contribute, Treasury officials don't try to identify or punish the donors. Most donations are anonymous, and many letters are from clergy, following up confessions taken at deathbeds.

Many contributions are sent by citizens who have resolved to start anew in life by righting past wrongs, but some are more grudging. In 2004, one donor wrote, "Dear Internal Revenue Service, I have not been able to sleep at night because I cheated on last year's income tax. Enclosed find a cashier's check for $1,000. If I still can't sleep, I'll send you the balance."

• • •

"APPARATUS FOR OBTAINING CRIMINAL CONFESSIONS"

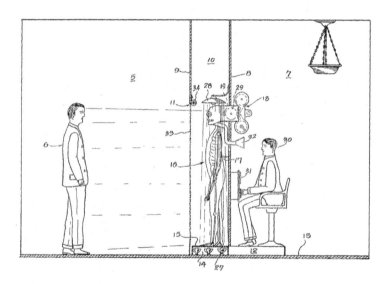

This one leaves me speechless. Helene Adelaide Shelby was unhappy with the low rate of criminal confessions, so in 1927 she invented a solution. The police put their suspect into the darkened chamber on the left, and he finds himself facing a floodlit human skeleton with glowing red eyes. The skeleton asks questions (via a megaphone in the mouth), and the suspect's reactions are recorded by a camera and a microphone in the skull.

The effect produces "a state of mind calculated to cause him, if guilty, to make confession." I'll bet. What if he's innocent?

• • •

COUCH LOGIC

Your vote will make a difference only if it breaks a tie or creates one.

This is very unlikely to be the case.

So why vote?

• • •

A GLASS DARKLY

Robert Browning spent seven years composing *Sordello*, a 40,000-word narrative poem about strife between Guelphs and Ghibellines in 13th-century Italy. It was not received well.

Tennyson said, "There were only two lines in it that I understood, and they were both lies: 'Who will may hear Sordello's story told' and 'Who would has heard Sordello's story told.'"

Thomas Carlyle wrote, "My wife has read through 'Sordello' without being able to make out whether 'Sordello' was a man, or a city, or a book."

Douglas Jerrold opened the book while convalescing from an illness and began to fear that his mind had been destroyed. "O God, I AM an idiot!" he cried, sinking back onto the sofa. He pressed the book on his wife and sister; when Mrs. Jerrold said, "I don't understand what this man means; it is gibberish," her husband exclaimed, "Thank God, I am NOT an idiot!"

In Walter Besant's 1895 novel *The Golden Butterfly*, one character spends eight hours trying to penetrate Browning's poetry. "His eyes were bloodshot, his hair was pushed in disorder about his head, his cheeks were flushed, his hands were trembling, the nerves in his face were twitching. He looked about him wildly, and tried to collect his faculties. Then he arose, and solemnly cursed Robert Browning. He cursed him eating, drinking, and sleeping. And then he took all his volumes, and disposing them carefully in the fireplace, set light to them. 'I wish,' he said, 'that I could put the poet there too.'"

Another (apocryphal) story tells of a puzzled friend who asked Browning the meaning of one of his poems. "When I wrote it, only God and I knew," the poet replied. "Now, God alone knows!"

• • •

STICKEEN

One day in 1880 John Muir set out to explore a glacier in southeastern Alaska, accompanied by Stickeen, the dog belonging to his traveling companion. The day went well, but on their way back to camp they found their way blocked by an immense 50-foot crevasse crossed diagonally by a narrow fin of ice. After long deliberation Muir cut his way down to the fin, straddled it and worked his way perilously across, but Stickeen, who had shown dauntless courage throughout the day, could not be convinced to follow. He sought desperately for some other route, gazing fearfully into the gulf and "moaning and wailing as if in the bitterness of death." Muir called to him, pretended to march off, and finally ordered him sternly to cross the bridge. Miserably the dog inched down to the farther end and, "lifting his feet with the regularity and slowness of the vibrations of a seconds pendulum," crept across the abyss and scrambled up to Muir's side.

❝❝And now came a scene! 'Well done, well done, little

boy! Brave boy!' I cried, trying to catch and caress him; but he would not be caught. Never before or since have I seen anything like so passionate a revulsion from the depths of despair to exultant, triumphant, uncontrollable joy. He flashed and darted hither and thither as if fairly demented, screaming and shouting, swirling round and round in giddy loops and circles like a leaf in a whirlwind, lying down, and rolling over and over, sidewise and heels over head, and pouring forth a tumultuous flood of hysterical cries and sobs and gasping mutterings. When I ran up to him to shake him, fearing he might die of joy, he flashed off two or three hundred yards, his feet in a mist of motion; then, turning suddenly, came back in a wild rush and launched himself at my face, almost knocking me down, all the while screeching and screaming and shouting as if saying, 'Saved! saved! saved!' Then away again, dropping suddenly at times with his feet in the air, trembling and fairly sobbing. Such passionate emotion was enough to kill him. Moses' stately song of triumph after escaping the Egyptians and the Red Sea was nothing to it. Who could have guessed the capacity of the dull, enduring little fellow for all that most stirs this mortal frame? Nobody could have helped crying with him!

Thereafter, Muir wrote, "Stickeen was a changed dog. During the rest of the trip, instead of holding aloof, he always lay by my side, tried to keep me constantly in sight, and would hardly accept a morsel of food, however tempting, from any hand but mine. At night, when all was quiet about the camp-fire, he would come to me and rest his head on my knee with a look of devotion as if I were his god. And often as he caught my eye he seemed to be trying to say, 'Wasn't that an awful time we had together on the glacier?'"

•••

A FEW WORDS

At the climax of the 1934 film *The Black Cat*, Boris Karloff recites a "black mass" over a swooning Jacqueline Wells:

❝ *Cum grano salis. Fortis cadere cedere non potest. Humanum est errare. Lupis pilum mutat, non mentem. Magna est veritas et praevalebit. Acta exteriora indicant interiora secreta. Aequam memento rebus in arduis servare mentem. Amissum quod nescitur non amittitur. Brutum fulmen. Cum grano salis. Fortis cadere cedere non potest. Fructu, non foliis arborem aestima. Insanus omnes furere credit ceteros. Quem paenitet peccasse paene est innocens.*

This sounds marvelous in Karloff's portentous baritone, but it's weaker in translation:

❝ With a grain of salt. A brave man may fall, but he cannot yield. To err is human. The wolf may change his skin, but not his nature. Truth is mighty, and will prevail. External actions show internal secrets. Remember when life's path is steep to keep your mind even. The loss that is not known is no loss at all. Heavy thunder. With a grain of salt. A brave man may fall, but he cannot yield. By fruit, not by leaves, judge a tree. Every madman thinks everybody mad. Who repents from sinning is almost innocent.

He might have added *Omnia dicta fortiora si dicta Latina*: "Everything sounds more impressive in Latin."

•••

DEAD BARGAIN

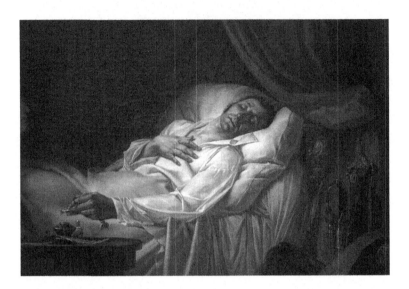

On my deathbed I exact a promise from you. Then I die, and you ignore the promise. Most of us would feel that this is wrong, but why? If I no longer exist, then who is wronged by your omission?

Similarly, it seems wrong to disparage the dead, or to mistreat a corpse. But why? Can we have a moral obligation to a person who doesn't exist? Do the dead have rights?

"The dead, if they exist at all, are so much dust," writes philosopher George Pitcher. "How is it possible for so much dust to be wronged?"

• • •

I CONTAIN MULTITUDES

OPERAS is the plural of OPERA, which is the plural of OPUS.

• • •

COVERUP

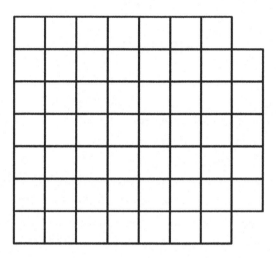

Two squares have been removed from this 8×7 rectangle. Can the remaining 54 squares be tiled orthogonally with 18 3×1 tiles?

(See Answers and Solutions)

• • •

UNQUOTE

"Tragedy is when I cut my finger. Comedy is when you fall into an open sewer and die."

— Mel Brooks

• • •

UNIVERSALLY CHILLY

-40° Celsius = -40° Fahrenheit

• • •

HIGHER THINGS

On a television show, Eddie Fisher complained to George S. Kaufman that women refused to date him because he looked so young. Kaufman considered this and replied:

"Mr. Fisher, on Mount Wilson there is a telescope that can magnify the most distant stars up to 24 times the magnification of any previous telescope. This remarkable instrument was unsurpassed until the construction of the Mount Palomar telescope, an even more remarkable instrument of magnification. Owing to advances and improvements in optical technology, it is capable of magnifying the stars to four times the magnification and resolution of the Mount Wilson telescope. Mr. Fisher, if you could somehow put the Mount Wilson telescope *inside* the Mount Palomar telescope, you *still* wouldn't be able to detect my interest in your problem."

• • •

"A GOOD BARGAIN"

❝A story is told of Sheridan, himself an Irishman, that one day, when coming back from shooting with an empty bag, he did not like to go home completely empty, and seeing a number of ducks in a pond, and a man or farmer leaning on a rail watching them, Sheridan said, 'What will you take for a shot at the ducks?'

'Well,' he said, 'I will take half a sovereign.'

'Done!' said Sheridan, and he fired into middle of the flock, killing a dozen. 'I am afraid you made a bad bargain!'

'I don't know,' said the man: 'they weren't mine.'

—*Tit-Bits From All the Most Interesting Books, Periodicals and Newspapers in the World*, Oct. 29, 1881

• • •

HEARING PLACES

Architect Stedman Whitwell thought it illogical and confusing that different towns sometimes have the same name. He suggested assigning a unique name to each location based on its latitude and longitude. He published this table in the New Harmony, Ind., *Gazette* in 1826:

	1	2	3	4	5	6	7	8	9	0
Latitude . . . . . . a	e	i	o	u	y	ee	ei	ie	ou
Longitude . . . . . b	d	f	k	l	m	n	p	r	t

Insert an S to indicate south latitude and a V for west longitude; omit them for north and east. Thus New Harmony (38°11'N, 87°55'W) would be rechristened Ipba Veinul; New York would be Otke Notive, Washington D.C. Feili Neivul, and Pittsburgh Otfu Veitoup.

What these names lack in poetry they make up in utility: A traveler given the name of a town can immediately infer its location. Unfortunately, Whitwell's scheme never caught on—and today the United States has 28 Springfields, 29 Clintons, and 30 Franklins.

• • •

A NEW DAY

Early on the morning of May 13, 1862, a lookout on the U.S.S. *Onward* spotted a Confederate steamer heading out of Charleston Harbor directly toward the Union blockade. Commander F.J. Nickels was about to fire when he saw that the steamer was flying a white flag. "The steamer ran alongside and I immediately boarded her, hauled down [the] flag of truce, and hoisted the American ensign, and found that it was the steamer *Planter*, of Charleston, and had successfully run past the forts and escaped."

The transport ship's pilot, Robert Smalls, had resolved to escape slavery by steaming out to the Union warships blockading his city. When the ship's white officers had gone ashore that night, he directed his eight fellow slaves to fire up the boilers and guided the ship to a nearby wharf, where they collected their families. Then Smalls donned the captain's hat and coat and gave two long and one short blasts on the whistle as they neared Fort Sumter, as he had seen the captain do. The sentry sent him on his way. As he made for the Union fleet three miles away, he put up one of his wife's bedsheets as a flag of truce.

Harper's Weekly called the theft "one of the most daring and heroic adventures since the war commenced." In his *Naval History of the Civil War*, Union admiral David Dixon wrote, "The taking out of the 'Planter' would have done credit to anyone, but the cleverness with which the whole affair was conducted deserves more than a passing notice."

Smalls was given a monetary reward for the captured *Planter* and went on to serve in the South Carolina legislature and the U.S. House of Representatives. When Abraham Lincoln asked why he had stolen the ship, he said simply, "Freedom."

• • •

CHARACTER STUDY

Story magazine nearly foundered for a lack of Ws. The publishers, Whit Burnett and Martha Foley, lived on Majorca, and their Spanish printer's character set could not accommodate their English prose.

They bought some supplementary Ws from a Madrid foundry, but the new type was distractingly sharp on the page. So the printer advised them to "make those new letters old."

"We sandpapered those Ws," wrote Foley, "we stamped on them, we hammered them and hurled them around to give them in an hour all the wear and tear the printer's other type had endured for many years. We finally subdued them so that they lost most of their prominence. But I have been W-conscious ever since."

• • •

FAIR POINT

❝'My dearest Maria,' wrote a recently-married husband to his wife. She wrote back, 'Dearest, let me correct either your grammar or your morals. You address me, "My dearest Maria." Am I to suppose you have other dear Marias?'

—*The Illinois Farmer,* June 1863

• • •

IN A WORD

boanthropy
n. the delusion that one is an ox

immiserization
n. the act of making or becoming progressively more
   miserable

burgh-bote
n. a tax for the repair of fortresses

jeofail
n. a lawyer's mistake

• • •

BAD FRIDAY

On July 3, 1863, 20-year-old Pennsylvania seamstress Ginnie
Wade was kneading dough in her sister's kitchen when a bullet
pierced the door behind her and passed through her heart, killing her instantly.

She was the only civilian casualty of the Battle of Gettysburg.

• • •

SENIOR CITIZEN

Paul Erdös claimed to be two and a half billion years old.

"When I was a child, the Earth was said to be two billion
years old," he said. "Now scientists say it's four and a half billion.
So that makes me two and a half billion."

• • •

LIGHTNING RODS

On April 18, 1926, Sinclair Lewis mounted the pulpit of a Kansas City church, took out his watch, and defied God to prove his existence within 10 minutes by striking him dead.

God spared him.

George Bernard Shaw had once made the same challenge but gave God only three minutes. "I am a very busy man," he said.

• • •

A BLINDFOLD BULLSEYE

In 1908, German novelist Ferdinand H. Grautoff published *Banzai!*, a curiously prescient account of a war between Japan and the United States. Japan deals a surprise defeat to unprepared American troops, who rally to repulse them:

❝❝Our splendid regiments could not be checked, so eager were they to push forward, and they succeeded in storming one of the enemy's positions after the other along the mountainside. At last the enemy began to retreat, and the thunder of the cannon was again and again drowned in the frenzied cheers. General MacArthur was continually receiving at his headquarters reports of fresh victories in the front and on both wings.

Note the name of the American commander. Grautoff gives no clue to his inspiration, but in an introduction he writes, "All the incidents we had observed on the dusty highway of History, and passed by with indifference, had been sure signs of the coming catastrophe."

• • •

VERSE

I thought I knew I knew it all,
But now I must confess,
The more I know I know I know,
I know I know the less.

—Anonymous

• • •

BOW TIE

On Oct. 27, 1917, violinist Mischa Elman and pianist Leopold Godowsky attended the first U.S. performance of 16-year-old violin prodigy Jascha Heifetz at Carnegie Hall.

At the intermission, Elman wiped his brow and said, "It's awfully hot in here." Godowsky said, "Not for pianists!"

• • •

HAND COUNT

Suppose we fill Yankee Stadium with 50,000 people and ask them to spend the day shaking hands with one another.

Prove that, at the end of the day, at least two participants will have shaken hands with the same number of people.

(See Answers and Solutions)

• • •

A TALL TAIL

As skywatchers prepared for the return of Halley's comet in 1910, their excitement turned to trepidation when astronomer Camille Flammarion warned that cyanogen gas in the comet's tail could poison the atmosphere. The *New York Times* reported growing alarm among astronomers and warned, "Prof. Flammarion is of the opinion that the cyanogen gas would impregnate the atmosphere and possibly snuff out all life on the planet." The *Washington Post* quoted astronomer Henri Deslandres that the comet might cause torrential rains; his colleague D.J. McAdam warned that "Disease and death have frequently been ascribed to the admixture of cometary gases with the air."

As the fateful date approached, an ad appeared in a South African newspaper: "Gentleman having secured several cylinders of oxygen and having bricked up a capacious room wishes to meet others who would share the expense for Wednesday night. Numbers strictly limited." In Texas, salesmen went door to door selling "comet pills" and leather inhalers. In Germany, anxious residents began wearing comet hats and carrying comet umbrellas.

On the evening of May 18, as Earth passed into the comet's tail, hundreds marched in a candlelight parade in San Juan, and prayer vigils were held in St. Petersburg churches and on the hilltops around Mexico City. In Lexington, Ky., excited citizens held all-night services, "praying and singing to prepare . . . [to] meet their doom."

Nothing happened. Well, nearly nothing: In Towaco, N.J., two men had offered to pay $10 for the best description of the event as viewed from Walkman Mountain. When the town's weary residents returned from their vigil, they found their chicken coops empty.

• • •

THE BETTER MAN

In 1822, frontiersman Hugh Glass joined a corps of 100 "enterprising young men" to ascend the Missouri River on a fur-trapping expedition. At the Grand River he was attacked by a grizzly bear; he and his companions managed to kill it, but Glass was badly mauled. The expedition's leader offered $40 for volunteers to remain with Glass until he died or could travel. The two men who accepted this charge, John Fitzgerald and Jim Bridger, waited a short interval and then simply took Glass' belongings and rejoined the expedition, reporting that they'd buried the body.

Glass awoke mutilated, alone, and unprovisioned 200 miles from the nearest settlement. He crawled south for six weeks, foraging on berries, roots, and the carcasses of buffalo, before he reached the Cheyenne River, where he fashioned a raft and floated to Fort Kiowa on the Missouri. Then he set out to seek revenge.

He found Bridger on the Yellowstone near the mouth of the Bighorn River, and decided to spare him because of his youth (Bridger had been only 17 when he'd abandoned Glass). He found Fitzgerald at Fort Atkinson, where he was serving as a private in the Sixth Infantry. Trapper George Yount recounts the climax:

> **“**Glass found the recreant individual, who had so cruelly deserted him, when he lay helpless & torn so shockingly by the Grizzly Bear—He also there recovered his favorite Rifle—To the man he only addressed himself as he did to the boy—'Go false man & answer to your own conscience & to your God;—I have suffered enough in all reason by your perfidy—You was well paid to have remained with me until I should be able to walk—You promised to do so—or to wait my death & decently bury my remains—I heard the bargain—Your shameful perfidy & heartless cruelty—but enough—Again I say, settle the matter with your own conscience & your God.'

He told Fitzgerald's commanding officer, “I reckon the skunk ain't worth shooting after all.”

PART TWO

GOATS, TORNADOES, *and* OLIVER WENDELL HOLMES

WISE CRACKS

In 1998, California physician Donald L. Unger wrote to the editors of *Arthritis & Rheumatism* to report a "50-year controlled study by one participant." His mother had told him that cracking his knuckles would lead to arthritis, so for 50 years the science-minded Unger had cracked the knuckles of his left hand at least twice a day, more than 36,500 times in all, and left the right uncracked as a control. After 50 years he found no arthritis in either hand and no differences between the two hands.

"This result calls into question whether other parental beliefs, e.g., the importance of eating spinach, are also flawed," Unger wrote. "Further investigation is likely warranted."

The editors invited a response from Robert L. Swezey, who had published an earlier investigation in the *Western Journal of Medicine*. Swezey said that his own study had been inspired when his 12-year-old son's grandmother had warned him that cracking his knuckles would cause arthritis. "It is now 22 years later and he continues to enjoy frequent KC without manifestations or evidence of arthritis."

With motherly advice thrown into doubt, Swezey wondered whether knuckle cracking might even prevent osteoarthritis. "The possible utilization of KC by managed care providers as an economic, noninvasive, home preventative treatment for arthritis of the hands should be given further consideration," he concluded. "A clear distinction between hand wringing related to managed care procedures and therapeutic KC will have to be made."

• • •

THE OTHER SIDE

An episode from the German trenches, August 1915, from ar-tilleryman Herbert Sulzbach's 1935 memoir *With the German Guns*:

> 66 One of the next starlit summer nights, a decent Land-wehr chap came up suddenly and said to 2/Lt Reinhardt, 'Sir, it's that Frenchie over there singing again so wonder-ful.' We stepped out of the dug-out into the trench, and quite incredibly, there was a marvellous tenor voice ring-ing out through the night with an aria from *Rigoletto*. The whole company were standing in the trench listening to the 'enemy,' and when he had finished, applauding so loud that the good Frenchman must certainly have heard it and is sure to have been moved by it in some way or other as much as we were by his wonderful singing.

"Musical compositions, it should be remembered, do not inhabit certain countries, certain museums, like paintings and statues," wrote Henri Rabaud. "The Mozart Quintet is not shut up in Salzburg: I have it in my pocket."

• • •

MORE AMUSING INDEXES

From Oliver Wendell Holmes' *The Poet at the Breakfast-Table*, 1872:

Act to make the poor rich by making the rich poorer, 3

Ankle, wonderful effects of breaking a bone in the, 114

Batrachian reservoir (frog-pond in vulgar speech), the palladium of our city, 369

Biography, penalties of being its subject, 191 et seq.

Common virtues of humanity not to be confiscated to the use of any one creed, 360

House-flies mysterious creatures, 288

Ideas often improve by transplantation, 171

Intellects, one story, two story, three story, 50

Jests distress some people, 289

Justice, an algebraic x, 317

Life a fatal complaint, and contagious, 395

Limitations, human, not to be transferred to the Infinite, 319

Millionaires cannot be exterminated, 5

Non-clerical minds, hopeful for the future of the race, 302

Old people almost wish to lose their blessings for the pleasure of remembering them, 385

Poem, is it hard work to write one?, 111

Power, we have no respect for as such, 317

Private property in thought hard to get and keep, 356

Ribbon in button-hole pleases the author, 322

Rigorists, mellowing, better than tightening liberals, 19

Tattooing with the belief of our tribe while we are in our cradles, 384

Traditionalists eliminate cause and effect from the domain of morals, 265

And from Robert Burton's *Anatomy of Melancholy*, 1621:

Atheists described, 705

Baseness of birth no disparagement, 509

Beer censured, 145

Black eyes best, 519

Blow on the head cause of melancholy, 247

Confidence in his physician half a cure, 392

Crocodiles jealous, 629

Eunuchs why kept, and where, 642

Fishes in love, 493

Great men most part dishonest, 636

Guts described, 96

Hell where, 318

How oft 'tis fit to eat in a day, 307

Ignorance the mother of devotion, 678

Man the greatest enemy to man, 84

Old folks apt to be jealous, 632

Poets why poor, 203

Salads censured, 145

Step-mother, her mischiefs, 241

Venison a melancholy meat, 142

Why good men are often rejected, 415

Why fools beget wise children, wise men fools, 139, 140

The *New York Times Book Review* called Burton's index "a readerly pleasure in itself."

• • •

GRAVE MATTERS

In 1554 Sir James Hales drowned himself. The coroner returned a verdict of *felo de se*, meaning that Sir James was guilty of the felony of self-murder. His estate was forfeited to the crown, which planned to award it to one Cyriac Petit. Sir James' widow, Margaret, contested this. So the case turned on the question whether the grounds for forfeiture had occurred during Sir James' lifetime: Had his suicide occurred during his life, or after his death?

Margaret Hales' counsel argued that one can't be guilty of suicide while one is still living, practically by definition, so self-murder shouldn't be classed as a felony: "He cannot be *felo de se* till the death is fully consummate, and the death precedes the felony and the forfeiture."

But Petit's counsel argued that part of the act of suicide lies in planning to do it, which certainly occurs during life: "The act consists of three parts: the first is the imagination, which is a reflection or meditation of the mind, whether or not it is convenient for him to destroy himself, and what way it can be done; the second is the resolution, which is a determination of the mind to destroy himself; the third is the perfection, which is the execution of what the mind had resolved to do. And of all the parts, the doing of the act is the greatest in the judgment of our law, and it is in effect the whole."

The court ruled for Petit, finding that Sir James had killed himself during his lifetime: "The forfeiture shall have relation to the time the original offence began which caused the death, and that was the throwing himself into the water, which was done in his lifetime and this act was felony. That which caused the death may be said to be feloniously done. The felony is attributed to the act, which act is always done by a living man; for,

Brown said, Sir James Hales was dead, and how came he by his death? It may be answered by drowning; and who drowned him? Sir James Hales; and when did he this? It can be answered, in his lifetime. So that Sir James Hales being alive caused Sir James Hales to be dead, and the act of the living man caused the death of the dead man."

The case is remembered, and not charitably, in the churchyard scene in *Hamlet*:

First Clown: Give me leave. Here lies the water; good: here stands the man; good; if the man go to this water, and drown himself, it is, will he, nill he, he goes,—mark you that; but if the water come to him and drown him, he drowns not himself: argal, he that is not guilty of his own death shortens not his own life.

Second Clown: But is this law?

First Clown: Ay, marry, is't; crowner's quest law.

• • •

MEMORABLE DEDICATIONS

By Franklin Pierce Adams, in *Overset*, 1922:

To
Herbert Bayard Swope
without whose friendly
aid and counsel every
line in this book was
written.

By Francis Hackett, in *The Invisible Censor*, 1921:

To
my wife

Signe Toksvig
whose lack of interest
in this book has been my
constant desperation.

By Benjamin Disraeli, in *Vivian Grey*, 1826:

To
The Best and Greatest of Men
I dedicate these volumes.
He for whom it was intended will accept and
appreciate the compliment;
Those for whom it was not intended will —
do the same.

By John Burroughs, in *Bird and Bough*, 1906:

To
the kinglet
that sang in my evergreens in October and
made me think it was May.

By Jerome K. Jerome, in *Idle Thoughts of an Idle Fellow*, 1886:

To the very dear and well beloved Friend of my prosperous
and evil days.—To the friend, who, though in the early stages
of our acquaintanceship, he did ofttimes disagree with me,
has since come to be my very warmest comrade. To the friend
who, however often I may put him out, never (now) upsets me
in revenge. To the friend who, treated with marked coldness
by all the female members of my household, and regarded
with suspicion by my very dog, nevertheless, seems day by

day to be more drawn by me, and in return, to more and more impregnate me with the odour of his friendship. To the friend who never tells me of my faults, never wants to borrow money, and never talks about himself. To the companion of my idle hours, the soother of my sorrows, the confidant of my joys and hopes, my oldest and strongest Pipe, this little volume is gratefully and affectionately dedicated.

• • •

BALL JUGGLING

In a solar eclipse, the moon casts its shadow on Earth. In a lunar eclipse, Earth casts its shadow on the moon.

Solar eclipses are more common than lunar eclipses, but we tend to have the opposite impression. Why?

(See Answers and Solutions)

• • •

LATE ACCEPTANCE

In 1832, at age 19, Giuseppe Verdi applied to study at the Milan Conservatory and was rejected.

In 1898, at the end of his career, he learned that the conservatory had decided to rename itself the Giuseppe Verdi Conservatorium.

"My God, this was all that was lacking to plague the soul of a poor devil like me who desires only to be serene and to die serenely!" he wrote to his publisher. "No, sir! Even this isn't allowed me! What wrong have I done that I should be tormented like this?"

That's not quite fair. He had been four years over the age limit and a foreigner to the state of Lombardy-Venetia, where the school was located. But he remembered it as "a Conservatorium that (I do not exaggerate) tried to kill me, and whose memory I should try to escape."

• • •

"THE DECLARATION OF INDEPENDENCE IN AMERICAN"

❝ When things get so balled up that the people of a country got to cut loose from some other country, and go it on their own hook, without asking no permission from nobody, excepting maybe God Almighty, then they ought to let everybody know why they done it, so that everybody can see they are not trying to put nothing over on nobody.

All we got to say on this proposition is this: first, me and you is as good as anybody else, and maybe a damn sight better; second, nobody ain't got no right to take away none of our rights; third, every man has got a right to live, to come and go as he pleases, and to have a good time whichever way he likes, so long as he don't interfere with nobody else. That any government that don't give a man them rights ain't worth a damn; also, people ought to choose the kind of government they want themselves, and nobody else ought to have no say in the matter. That whenever any government don't do this, then the people have got a right to give it the bum's rush and put in one that will take care of their interests. Of course, that don't mean having a revolution every day like them South American yellowbellies, or every time some jobholder goes to work and does something he ain't got no business to do. It is better to stand a little graft, etc., than to have revolutions all the time, like them coons, and any man that wasn't a anarchist or one of them I.W.W.'s would say the same. But when things get so bad that a man ain't hardly got no rights at all no more, but you might almost call him a slave, then everybody ought to get together and throw the grafters out, and put in new ones who won't carry on so high and steal so much, and then watch them. This is the proposition the people of these Colonies is up against, and they have got tired of it, and won't stand it no more.

—H.L. Mencken, *The American Language*, 1921

• • •

CLOUDY

All rational beings believe in their own existence, whether or not they actually exist. Sherlock Holmes believes that he exists, but he is wrong. God too believes in his own existence—and his omniscience makes it impossible that he is mistaken. Therefore God exists.

On the other hand: Perfection is essential to godhood, and a perfect God must be perfectly virtuous. But virtue implies overcoming pain, fear, and temptation, and a God who is subject to these ills is less perfect than one who is not. Thus perfection is impossible, and God cannot exist.

Asked what he would say to God on Judgment Day, Bertrand Russell said, "Not enough evidence, God! Not enough evidence!"

• • •

WORLDLY WISE

Proverbs from around the world:

- A shroud has no pockets. (Scotland)
- No one is a blacksmith at birth. (Namibia)
- The absent always bears the blame. (Netherlands)
- One cannot make soup out of beauty. (Estonia)
- Bad is called good when worse happens. (Norway)
- When the mouse laughs at the cat, there is a hole. (Gambia)
- Under trees it rains twice. (Switzerland)
- Everyone is foolish until they buy land. (Ireland)
- Every head is a world. (Cuba)
- The only victory over love is flight. (France)
- Don't look where you fell, but where you slipped. (Liberia)
- Many lose when they win, and others win when they lose. (Germany)

And "It is not economical to go to bed early to save the candles if the result is twins." (China)

• • •

TALL ORDER

From Lewis Carroll:

Men over 5 feet high are numerous.

Men over 10 feet high are not numerous.

Therefore men over 10 feet high are not over 5 feet high.

• • •

SELF-STORAGE

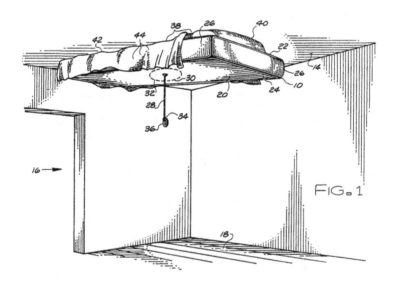

I like this one: If you fill your air mattress with helium you can keep it on the ceiling.

William Calderwood's 1989 brainstorm automatically increases the floor space in a small apartment. When you get up in the morning the bed floats to the ceiling, and you can spend the day roller-skating beneath it. Then at bedtime you pull it down again by the tether. Best of all, you never have to make the bed, because no one will ever see it!

• • •

IN A WORD

abuccinate
v. to announce with a flourish of trumpets

mushfaker
n. a repairer of umbrellas

latibulate
v. to hide oneself in a corner

afterwit
n. knowledge gained too late to do any good

• • •

RELATIVELY SPEAKING

The Pont Neuf is the oldest bridge across the Seine. *Pont neuf* means "new bridge."

• • •

"A MUCH TRAVELED GOAT"

❝About the year 1772 there died at Mile End, England, a well informed goat, if traveling and seeing the world would make it so. It twice circumnavigated the globe; first in the discovery ship *Dolphin*, with Captain Wallis, and afterward in the ship *Endeavorer*, commanded by the celebrated Captain Cook. The *Dolphin* sailed from England August 22, 1766, and returned May 20, 1768. It visited many lands, including numerous islands of the Pacific, on this voyage. The goat did not remain ashore very long, for the *Endeavorer* sailed from Plymouth August 25, 1768. The vessel touched at Maderia, doubled Cape Horn, spent six months along the coast of New Zealand, and visited many other strange countries. It got back to England June 12, 1771. In the three years Cook lost thirty of his eighty-five men, but the goat returned in apparent good health. Arrangements were made to admit her to the privileges of one of the government homes for sailors, but she did not live to enjoy them. She wore a silver collar, with a Latin inscription prepared by Dr. Samuel Johnson.

—Albert William Macy, *Curious Bits of History*, 1912

• • •

JEROME

On Sept. 8, 1863, two boys discovered a legless man struggling on the beach at Sandy Cove, Nova Scotia. Coughing violently and suffering from exposure, he appeared to be in his late teens or early 20s, and he seemed unable or unwilling to respond to their inquiries.

As the villagers nursed him back to health they found him angry and gloomy by nature, keeping his identity to himself. Rumors began to circulate: He was a Civil War veteran, a pirate, a spy, an exiled Habsburg, a murderer, a mutineer. His soft hands seemed to suggest high birth, but he had been found with only a tin box of hardtack and a jug of water, and he spoke neither English, Spanish, French, Italian, nor Latin. His legs had apparently been amputated by a skilled surgeon. As all attempts to communicate with him were unsuccessful, he came to be known simply as Jerome, after a response he had mumbled when asked his name.

That's the whole story. For the next 50 years Jerome was lodged with various local families, maintaining his silence despite endless inquiries from curiosity seekers. His identity was never discovered. When he died, finally, on April 15, 1912, the *Halifax Morning Chronicle* wrote, "The people in this vicinity have given up the solving of the great mystery that closed today in death, thus ending one of the greatest secrets that ever occurred on this continent."

● ● ●

A CHANGE OF KEY

$5 \times 55 \times 555 = 152625$
remains true if each digit is increased by 1:
$6 \times 66 \times 666 = 263736$

● ● ●

THE PERILS OF JOURNALISM

❝ An accident, the consequences of which are expected to be fatal, took place at Cannes on Sunday last. A M. Despleschin, of Nice, had announced his intention of making an ascent in a balloon, and two gentlemen, M. Hardy, of Cannes, and M.A. de Sorr, a literary man from Paris, had made arrangements to accompany him. These two gentlemen had taken their seats in the car, M. Despleschin not having yet entered it, when some person in the crowd, anxious to see the balloon start, cried out 'Let go.' The man who held the ropes, thinking that the order had come from the aeronaut, obeyed, and the balloon rose rapidly into the clouds, and disappeared. M. Hardy and M. de Sorr are both entirely ignorant of the management of a balloon, and it is feared that they have been carried out to sea. Up to the 2d. no intelligence had been received of them.

—*Times*, May 9, 1854

• • •

ANTIGRAMS

An antigram is a word or phrase whose letters can be rearranged to produce an opposite meaning:

ABET = BEAT
ABOMINABLE = BON, AMIABLE
ADVERSARIES = ARE ADVISERS
ANTAGONIST = NOT AGAINST
BOASTING = IT'S NO GAB
COMMENDATION = AIM TO CONDEMN
CONVENTIONAL = I VOTE NON-CLAN
DEFIANT = FAINTED
DEMONIACAL = A DOCILE MAN
FASHIONABLE = FINE? HA, A SLOB!
FILLED = ILL-FED

FORBID = BID FOR
HIBERNIANS = BANISH ERIN
HOME RUN HITTER = I'M NOT RUTH HERE
HONESTLY = ON THE SLY
HONOREES = NO HEROES
INDISCRIMINATE = DISCERN AIM IN IT
INNERMOST = I NEST ON RIM
LEGION = LONE GI
NOMINATE = I NAME NOT
PROSPEROUS = POOR PURSES
ROUSING = SOURING
THOMAS A. EDISON = TOM HAS NO IDEAS
TIMBERLESS = TREES, LIMBS
WOMANISH = HOW MAN IS

Without any rearrangement at all, IMPARTIALLY can be read as I'M PART, I ALLY. And DEFENCE is DE-FENCE!

• • •

UNQUOTE

"There are three rules for writing the novel. Unfortunately, no one knows what they are."—Somerset Maugham

• • •

EMPTIED NEST

Solve for x:

$$\sqrt{x + \sqrt{x + \sqrt{x}\ldots}} = 2$$

(See Answers and Solutions)

• • •

INDOORS AND OUT

The world's smallest country is smaller than the world's largest buildings.

Vatican City occupies 44 hectares, or about 4,736,120 square feet.

The Pentagon, by comparison, has a total floor area of 6,636,360 square feet.

• • •

"THE VIPER"

Yet another great truth I record in my verse,
That some Vipers are venomous, some the reverse;
A fact you may prove if you try,
By procuring two Vipers and letting them bite;
With the first you are only the worse for a fright,
But after the second you die.

—Hilaire Belloc

• • •

INDIAN WINTER

Convinced that other newspapers were stealing his news items, the publisher of the Kennett Square (Pa.) *Kennett News and Advertiser* invented a story about two Indians named Yrotss Ihte Lotsi and Ffutsse Lpoepre Htognil Aets.

Sure enough, the *West Chester Daily Local News* rewrote the piece for its Jan. 27, 1940, issue. Read the names backward.

• • •

FEEDBACK

In 1860, Abraham Lincoln received this letter from a Pete Muggins in Fillmore, La.:

> ❝God damn your god damned old Hellfired god damned soul to hell god damn you and goddam your god damned family's god dammed hellfired god damned soul to hell and god damnnation god damn them and god damn your god damn friends to hell god damn their god damned souls to damnation.

"Quarrel not at all," Lincoln wrote on another occasion. "No man resolved to make the most of himself can spare time for personal contention."

• • •

POSER

What's the difference between six dozen dozen and half a dozen dozen?

If you answered "nothing," reconsider.

• • •

POP QUIZ

Visiting London for the first time in 1912, Russian poet Samuil Marshak asked a man on the street, "Please, what is time?"

The man said, "That's a philosophical question. Why ask me?"

• • •

TWISTER VISION

Kansas farmer Will Keller was fleeing a tornado on June 22, 1928, when he turned at the door of his cyclone cellar and looked up:

66 To my astonishment I saw right up into the heart of the tornado. There was a circular opening in the center of the funnel, about 50 or 100 feet in diameter, and extending straight upward for a distance of at least one half mile, as best I could judge under the circumstances. The walls of this opening were of rotating clouds and the whole was made brilliantly visible by constant flashes of lightning which zigzagged from side to side. Had it not been for the lightning, I could not have seen the opening, not any distance into it anyway.

Only a handful of people have witnessed this sight and lived.

• • •

THEY GROW UP SO FAST

The day before yesterday, Timmy was 13 years old. Next year he'll be 16. What is his birthday, and what is today's date?

(See Answers and Solutions)

• • •

Q.E.D.

No cat has two tails.
Every cat has one tail more than no cat.
Therefore every cat has three tails.

• • •

QUICK THINKING

In summer 1940, Germany demanded access to Swedish telephone cables to send encoded messages from occupied Norway back to the homeland. Sweden acceded but tapped the lines and discovered that a new cryptographic system was being used. The *Geheimschreiber*, with more than 800 quadrillion settings, was conveying top-secret information but seemed immune to a successful codebreaking attack.

The Swedish intelligence service assigned mathematician Arne Beurling to the task, giving him only a pile of coded messages and no knowledge of the mechanism that had been used to encode them. But after two weeks alone with a pencil and paper he announced that the G-schreiber contained 10 wheels, with a different number of positions on each wheel, and described how a complementary machine could be built to decode the messages.

Thanks to his work, Swedish officials learned in advance of the impending invasion of the Soviet Union. Unfortunately, Stalin's staff disregarded their warnings.

"To this day no one knows exactly how Beurling reasoned during the two weeks he spent on the G-Schreiber," writes Peter Jones in his foreword to *The Codebreakers*, Bengt Beckman's account of the exploit. "In 1976 he was interviewed about his work by a group from the Swedish military, and became extremely irritated when pressed for an explanation. He finally responded, 'A magician does not reveal his tricks.' It seems the only clue Beurling ever offered was the remark, cryptic itself, that threes and fives were important."

• • •

SEA WAR

On the afternoon of June 21, 1818, the crew of the packet *Delia*, sailing between Boston and Hallowell, Maine, came upon a

struggle between a sea serpent and a large humpback whale, according to a statement sworn before a local justice of the peace.
From Henry Cheever's *The Whale and His Captors* (1850):

❝ The serpent threw up his tail from twenty-five to thirty feet in a perpendicular direction, striking the whale by it with tremendous blows rapidly repeated, which were distinctly heard and very loud for two or three minutes. They then both disappeared, moving in a west southwest direction, but after a few minutes reappeared in shore of the packet, and about under the sun, the reflection of which was so strong as to prevent their seeing so distinctly as at first, when the serpent's fearful blows with his tail were repeated and clearly heard as before. They again went down for a short time, and then came up to the surface under the packet's larboard quarter, the whale appearing first and the serpent in pursuit, who was again seen to shoot up his tail as before, which he held out of water some time, waving it in the air before striking, and at the same time, while his tail remained in this position, he raised his head fifteen or twenty feet, as if taking a view of the surface of the sea. After being seen in this position a few minutes, the serpent and whale again sunk and disappeared, and neither were seen after by any on board.

Sea serpents, it seems, tend to win these contests—the English barque *Pauline* witnessed a similar drubbing half a century later.

• • •

JUNK MAIL

After the San Francisco earthquake, James Jones wrote this letter on a detachable shirt collar and mailed it without postage to his son and daughter-in-law in New York:

66 Dear Wayland and Gussie: All safe but awfully scared. Frisco and hell went into partnership and hell came out winner—got away with the sack. Draw a line from Ft Mason along Van Ness Ave. to Market St., out Market to Dolores to Twentieth, thence to Harrison, 16th & Portrero Ave. R.R. Ave. to Channel St. and bay. Nearly everything east and north of this boundary line gone, and several blocks west of it, especially in Hayes Valley as far as Octavia St. from Golden Gate Ave. east. Fire is still burning on the northside but is checked in the Mission. I and a band of 40 or 50 volunteers formed a rope and bucket brigade, back-fired Dolores from Market to 19th, pulled down houses and blanketed westside Dolores and won a great victory. More with paper & stamps. James G. Jones. April 21st, 1906.

It was delivered. The post office had resolved to handle "everything, stamped or unstamped, as long as it had an address to which it could be sent," remembered William F. Burke, secretary to the city postmaster. When he made the rounds of camps, "the wonderful mass of communications that poured into the automobile was a study in the sudden misery that had overtaken the city. Bits of cardboard, cuffs, pieces of wrapping paper, bits of newspapers with an address on the margin, pages of books and sticks of wood all served as a means to let somebody in the outside world know that friends were alive and in need among the ruins."

At the close of the first day, "95 pouches of letters carrying mail composed of rags and tatters and odds and ends—and burdened with a weight of woe bigger than had ever left the city in a mail sack—were made up for dispatch. . . . It came to our knowledge later that not one piece of this mail that was properly addressed failed of delivery."

PART THREE

MOTHER'S DAY, BADGERS,
and
RUTHERFORD B. HAYES

OUT OF SIGHT

In 1915, after being cut off from his regiment in northern France, British Army private Patrick Fowler found his way to the farmhouse of Marie Belmont-Gobert in the German-occupied town of Bertry. He implored her to hide him, but she had space only in an oaken cupboard in the living room.

Incredibly, Fowler spent three years and nine months in a space 5.5 feet high and 20 inches deep while more than 20 German musketeers were billeted in the same house. "He was there at times when unsuspecting Germans were actually sitting around the fire in the same room," reported the *New York World* in 1927. "Often they came down to the ground floor quarters of the Belmont family and made coffee on the fire there."

The Germans even made periodic searches. "[A German captain] and his men sounded the walls and floors for secret hiding places, uttered awful threats," reported *Time*. "Mme. Belmont-Gobert only sat passive in her sitting room. At last the captain wrenched open the right-hand door of her large black armoire, snorted to see it divided into small shelves incapable of holding a rabbit, banged the right-hand door shut without opening the left-hand door, strode away."

The Germans finally left Bertry on Oct. 10, 1918, and Fowler returned to his unit. Nine years later, in recognition of her act, the French government granted Belmont-Gobert a pension, and Britain named her a Dame of the Order of the British Empire. The cupboard resides today in the King's Royal Hussars' Museum in Winchester.

• • •

ALL GREEK

In 1948, George Washington University doctoral student Ralph Alpher was working on a cosmology thesis under physicist George Gamow. As the paper took shape, "Gamow, with the usual twinkle in his eye, suggested that we add the name of Hans Bethe to an Alpher-Gamow letter to the editor of the *Physical Review*," listing the authors as Alpher-Bethe-Gamow.

Bethe agreed to join, and the result, now known as the αßγ paper, was published on April 1, 1948 ("believe it or not, a date not of our asking"). "The response was fascinating," Alpher later recalled, "ranging from feature articles, Sunday supplement stories, newspaper cartoons and voluminous mail from religious fundamentalists, to a packed audience of over 200, including members of the press, at the traditionally public (though usually not in this sense) 'defence' of the thesis."

Gamow added, "There was, however, a rumor that later, when the alpha, beta, gamma theory went temporarily on the rocks, Dr. Bethe seriously considered changing his name to Zacharias."

• • •

DISPATCH

"Don't waste your time on the branches small,"
Said the farmer to his son,
"But lay your axe at the root of the tree,
So your work is sooner done."

Then, like a good and obedient boy,
Not a word back did he say,

But he laid his axe at the root of the tree,
And went off and fished all day.

—Newton Mackintosh, *Precious Nonsense!*, 1895

• • •

IN A WORD

perendinate
v. to put off until the day after tomorrow

vaccimulgence
n. the milking of cows

philologaster
n. an incompetent philologist

apodyopsis
n. the act of imagining a person naked

• • •

SNAIL MAIL

Crouching in a Flanders trench in November 1917, 21-year-old
Walter Butler addressed a field service card to his fiancee Amy
to let her know he was safe.

She never received it. After the war Butler returned to England and the pair married, moved to London, and had a daughter. Eventually they divorced; Amy returned to her family home
while Walter remarried and led a career as a builder. She died in
1974 at age 81, he four years later at 82.

In February 2007, the card arrived. Their daughter, now an 86-year-old grandmother, received it.

"I am quite well," it said. "Letter follows at first opportunity. I have received no letter from you for a long time."

· · ·

"THE TWENTY-THIRD PSAUM"

6 6 The Lord is my Shepherd; my wants are a' kent; the pasture I lie on is growthie and green.

I follow by the lip o' the watirs o' Peace.

He heals and sterklie hauds my saul: and airts me, for his ain name's sake, in a' the fit-roads o' his holiness.

Aye, and though I bude gang throwe the howe whaur the deid-shadows fa', I'se fear nae skaith nor ill, for that yersel is aye aside me; yere rod and yere cruik they defend me.

My table ye hae plenish't afore the een o' my faes; my heid ye hae chrystit wi' oyle; my cup is teemin fu'!

And certes, tenderness and mercie sal be my fa' to the end o' my days; and syne I'se bide i' the hoose o' the Lord, for evir and evir mair!

—William Wye Smith, *The New Testament in Braid Scots*, 1904

· · ·

MATCHUPS

Titles of "in rem" condemnation cases, in which the government sues to justify the seizure of an asset:

- United States v. 11 1/4 Dozen Packages of Article Labeled in Part Mrs. Moffat's Shoo Fly Powders for Drunkenness, 40 F. Supp. 208 (W.D.N.Y. 1941)
- United States v. 2,116 Boxes of Boned Beef, etc., 726 F.2d 1481
- United States v. Approximately 64,695 Pounds of Shark Fins, 520 F.3d 976 (9th Cir. 2008)
- United States v. 2,507 Live Canary Winged Parakeets, 689 F. Supp. 1106 (S.D. Fla. 1988)
- United States v. One Lucite Ball Containing Lunar Material (One Moon Rock) and One Ten Inch by Fourteen Inch Wooden Plaque, 235 F. Supp. 2d 1367 (S.D. Fla. 2003)
- United States v. Article Consisting of 50,000 Cardboard Boxes More or Less, Each Containing One Pair of Clacker Balls, 413 F. Supp. 1281 (D. Wisconsin 1976)

In 1836 a flotilla of brandy casks washed ashore on the south coast of England, and an ownership dispute arose between a local property owner and the crown. Unfortunately for William IV, the case was recorded as The King v. Forty-Nine Casks of Brandy.

• • •

COUNTDOWN

There are exactly 10! seconds in six weeks.

• • •

MEMENTO

In 1798 Horatio Nelson's navy defeated a French fleet off the coast of Egypt. Captain Benjamin Hallowell, who helped to destroy the French flagship *L'Orient*, sent Nelson a macabre gift:

> My Lord,
> Herewith I send you a Coffin made of part of L'Orient's Main mast, that when you are tired of this Life you may be buried in one of your own Trophies—but may that period be far distant, is the sincere wish of your obedient and much obliged servant,
> Ben Hallowell

Nelson was indeed buried in it after his death in the Battle of Trafalgar in 1805.

• • •

"INSTANCE OF EXTRAORDINARY AFFECTION IN A BADGER"

❝The following circumstance is related in a letter to a friend from Chateau de Venours:—

'Two persons were on a short journey, and passing through a hollow way, a dog which was with them started a badger, which he attacked, and pursued, till he look shelter in a burrow under a tree. With some pains they hunted him out, and killed him. . . . Not having a rope, they twisted some twigs, and drew him along the road by turns. They had not proceeded far, when they heard a cry of an animal in seeming distress, and stopping to see from whence it proceeded, another badger approached them slowly. They at first threw stones at it, notwithstanding which it drew near, came up to the dead animal, began to lick it, and continued its mournful cry. The men, surprised at this, desisted from offering any further injury to it, and again drew the dead one along as before; when the living badger, determining not to quit its dead companion, lay down on it, taking it gently by one ear, and in that manner was drawn into the midst of the village; nor could dogs, boys, or men induce it to quit its situation by any means, and to their shame be it said, they had the inhumanity to kill it, and afterwards to burn it, declaring it could be no other than a witch.'

—Pierce Egan, *Sporting Anecdotes,*
Original and Selected, 1822

• • •

SIDELINE

In the 1890s an eminent Scot began to publish short popular science articles under an assumed name, for "the fun of seeing if he [could] make another reputation for himself."

He succeeded, publishing three articles in the *National Geographic* before the secret leaked out.

The pseudonym was H.A. Largelamb. Who was the man?

(See Answers and Solutions)

• • •

TRAVELING COMPANIONS

In 1848, Ellen and William Craft resolved to flee slavery, but they needed a way to get from Macon, Ga., to the free states in the north. William could never travel such a distance alone, but Ellen's skin was fair enough that she could pass for white. So she disguised herself as a white male cotton planter attended by William, her slave. (She had to pose as a man because a white woman would not have traveled alone with a male slave.) The two asked leave to be away for the holidays, the illiterate Ellen bound her arm in a sling to escape being asked to write, and they departed on Dec. 21. Over the next four days:

- Ellen found herself sitting next to a friend of her master on the train to Savannah. She feigned deafness to discourage his attempts to engage her in conversation.
- The captain of a steamer to Charleston complimented Ellen on her "very attentive boy" and warned him to shun the "cutthroat abolitionists" in the north.
- During the voyage a slave trader offered to buy William, and a military officer scolded Ellen for saying "thank you" to her slave.
- In South Carolina a ticket seller insisted on seeing proof that Ellen owned William. A passing captain intervened and sent them on their way.
- In a Virginia railway station a white woman confronted William, mistaking him for her own runaway slave.
- An officer in Baltimore threatened again to detain them without proof of ownership, but relented, telling a clerk, "He is not well, it is a pity to stop him."

On Dec. 25, after a journey of more than 800 miles, they arrived in Philadelphia:

    ❝ On leaving the station, my master—or rather my wife, as I may now say—who had from the commencement of the journey borne up in a manner that much surprised us both, grasped me by the hand, and said, 'Thank God, William, we are safe!' then burst into tears, leant upon me, and wept like a child. The reaction was fearful. So when we reached the house, she was in reality so weak and faint that she could scarcely stand alone. However, I got her into the apartments that were pointed out, and there we knelt down, on this Sabbath, and Christmas-day,—a day that will ever be memorable to us,—and poured out our heartfelt gratitude to God, for his goodness in enabling us to overcome so many perilous difficulties, in escaping out of the jaws of the wicked.

The Crafts went on a speaking tour of New England to share their story with abolitionists, then moved to England to evade recapture under the Fugitive Slave Act. They returned only in 1868, when they established a school in Georgia for newly freed slaves.

• • •

DREAMED UP

In composing a state map of New York in the 1930s, the General Drafting Company wanted to be sure that competing mapmakers would not simply copy its work. So the company's founder, Otto G. Lindberg, and his assistant, Ernest Alpers, scrambled their initials and placed the fictional town of Agloe at the intersection of two dirt roads in the Catskills north of Roscoe.

Several years later, they discovered Agloe on a Rand McNally map and confronted their competitor. But Rand was innocent: It had got the name from the county government, which had taken it from the Agloe General Store, which now occupied the intersection. The store had taken the name from a map by Esso, which had (apparently) copied it from Lindberg's map. Agloe had somehow clambered from imagination into reality.

Similarly, in 2001 editors placed a fake word in the *New Oxford American Dictionary* as a trap for other lexicographers who might steal their material. Fittingly, the word was *esquivalience*, "the willful avoidance of one's official responsibilities; the shirking of duties."

Sure enough, the word turned up at Dictionary.com (it's since been taken down), citing *Webster's New Millennium Dictionary*.

And as with Agloe, the invention has taken on a life of its own. *NOAD* editor Christine Lindberg, who coined *esquivalience*, told the *Chicago Tribune* that she finds herself using it regularly. "I especially like the critical, judgmental tone I can get out of it: 'Those esquivalient little wretches.' Sounds literate and nasty all in one breath. I like that."

• • •

FROM THE HEART

Banker James M. Fail repeatedly donated money to his alma mater, the University of Alabama, which he credited for his success in the business world. But he declined opportunities to give his name to an Alabama facility. "After all," he said, "who would want anything with the name 'Fail' on it?"

In 2008 he found a way to support the school and accept credit—he put his name on the visitors' locker room.

• • •

CASKET TROUBLE

❝ ❝ If Socrates died, he died either when he was alive or when he was dead. He did not die when he was alive—for then the same man would have been both living and dead. Nor when he was dead; for then he would have been dead twice. Therefore Socrates did not die.

—Sextus Empiricus, *Against the Physicists*

• • •

THE DEVIL'S GAME

Ms. C dies and goes to hell, where the devil offers a game of chance. If she plays today, she has a 1/2 chance of winning; if she plays tomorrow, the chance will be 2/3; and so on. If she wins, she can go to heaven, but if she loses she must stay in hell forever. When should she play?

The answer is not clear. If she waits a full year, her probability of winning will have risen to about 0.997268. At that point, waiting an additional day will improve her chances by only about 0.000007. But at stake is infinite joy, and 0.000007 multiplied by infinity is infinite. And the additional day spent waiting will contain (presumably) only a finite amount of torment. So it seems that the expected benefit from a further delay will always outweigh the cost.

"This logic might suggest that Ms. C should wait forever, but clearly such a strategy would be self-defeating," wrote Edward J. Gracely in proposing this conundrum in *Analysis* in 1988. "Why should she stay forever in a place in order to increase her chances of leaving it? So the question remains: what should Ms. C do?"

• • •

UNQUOTE

"Among the smaller duties of life I hardly know any one more important than that of not praising where praise is not due."—Sydney Smith

• • •

ONE SOLUTION

Beset with writer's block, Robert Benchley typed the word *The*, thinking it "as safe a start as any."

Then he left for an hour with friends.

On returning to his room he regarded the solitary word, alone on its expanse of blank paper.

He typed *hell with it* and "went out happily for the evening."

• • •

THE EARLY BIRD

Rutherford B. Hayes took the oath of office two days ahead of schedule, in a secret ceremony at the White House on March 3, 1877, attended by President Grant.

Hayes' opponent, Samuel Tilden, had won the popular vote but lost the electoral college, and rumors were circulating that he planned to claim the presidency for himself.

That didn't happen, and Hayes was inaugurated peacefully on March 5.

But, arguably, for those two days in March the United States had two presidents.

• • •

THE FIVE ROOMS

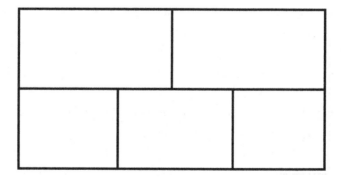

Here's the floor plan of a house with five rooms. Can you draw a continuous line that passes through each of the 16 wall segments once and once only? If it's possible, show how; if it's not, explain why.

(See Answers and Solutions)

• • •

SOTTO VOCE

❝ ❝ 'Wordsworth,' said Charles Lamb, 'one day told me that he considered Shakespeare greatly overrated. "There is an immensity of trick in all Shakespeare wrote," he said, "and people are taken in by it. Now if I had a mind I could write exactly like Shakespeare." So you see,' proceeded Charles Lamb quietly, 'it was only the mind that was wanting.'

—*Frank Leslie's Ten Cent Monthly*, December 1863

• • •

A XENOPHOBE'S GAZETTEER

Evangelical author Favell Lee Mortimer (1802-1878) set foot only twice outside England, but that didn't stop her from writing harrowing travel books for Victorian children. From *The Countries of Europe Described* (1850):

- "There are not nearly as many thieves in Wales as there are in England."
- "[On Easter] the streets of Petersburgh are filled with staggering, reeling drunkards."
- "Nothing useful is well done in Sweden."
- "It is dreadful to think what a number of murders are committed in Italy."
- "The Greeks do not know how to bring up their children."
- "A great many people have coughs in Vienna, because the east wind blows very cold."

- "Though the Portuguese are indolent, like the Spaniards, they are not so grave, and sad, and silent."
- "The Hungarians are much wilder people than the Germans; they are not industrious; they do not know how to make things; most of them cannot read or write."
- "The greatest fault of the Norwegians is drunkenness."
- "The Poles love talking, and they speak so loud they almost scream; and they are proud of this, and say that the Germans are dumb."
- "Denmark is flat, but not nearly as flat as Holland, nor as damp, nor as ugly."

"I do not mean to say that there are as many robbers in Sweden as in Sicily; there the robbers are seldom punished at all: in Sweden they are punished; but yet the rest of the people go on stealing."

• • •

R.I.P.

❝ ❝ A man was killed by a circular saw, and in his obituary notice it was stated that he was 'a good citizen, an upright man and an ardent patriot, but of limited information with regard to circular saws.'

—James Baird McClure, ed., *Entertaining Anecdotes From Every Available Source*, 1879

• • •

PULL!

Bicycles are great for exercising the lower body, but what about the back? In 1900 Louis S. Burbank had a bright idea—by mounting a pair of sculls on the frame, the modern cyclist can row his way to total fitness.

The levers are used for both pedaling and steering. The patent says nothing about brakes.

• • •

SEA LEGS

Commandant Louis Joseph Lahure has a singular distinction in military history—he defeated a navy on horseback.

Occupying Holland in January 1795, the French continental army learned that the mighty Dutch navy had been frozen into the ice around Texel Island. So Lahure and 128 men simply rode up to it and demanded surrender. No shots were fired.

• • •

RED MENACE

Driving habits of communists, according to J. Edgar Hoover:

- Driving alternately at high and low rates of speed.
- Entering a heavily traveled intersection on a yellow light, hoping to lose any follower or cause an accident.
- Turning corners at high rates of speed and stopping abruptly.
- Suddenly leaving a car and walking hurriedly down a one-way street in the direction in which vehicle traffic is prohibited.
- Entering a dark street in a residential area at night, making a sharp U-turn, cutting into a side alley, and extinguishing the car's lights.

- Driving to a rural area, taking a long walk in a field, then having another car meet them.
- Waiting until the last minute, then making a sharp left turn in front of oncoming traffic.
- Stopping at every filling station on the highway, walking around the car, always looking, then going on.

"Always there is the fear of being followed," he wrote in *Masters of Deceit* (1958). "One Party couple registered at a motel, then the husband parked the car several miles away. He walked back and climbed through a side window. Maybe in this way he would conceal his next night's lodging!"

• • •

NO THANKS

In June 1744, the College of William & Mary invited the Indians of the Six Nations to send six young men to be "properly" educated. They received this reply:

❝ ❝ We know that you highly esteem the kind of learning taught in those Colleges, and that the Maintenance of our young Men, while with you, would be very expensive to you. We are convinc'd, therefore, that you mean to do us Good by your Proposal; and we thank you heartily. But you, who are wise, must know that different Nations have different Conceptions of Things; and you will therefore not take it amiss if our Ideas of this kind of Education happen not to be the same with yours. We have had some Experience of it: Several of our young People were formerly brought up at the Colleges of the Northern Provinces; they were instructed in all your Sciences; but when they came back to us, they were bad Runners, ignorant of every means of living in the Woods, unable to bear either Cold or Hunger, knew neither how to build a Cabin, take a Deer, or kill an Enemy, spoke our Language imperfectly, were therefore neither fit for Hunters, Warriors, or Counsellors; they were totally good for nothing. We are, however, not the less oblig'd by your kind Offer, tho' we decline accepting it; and, to show our grateful Sense of it, if the Gentlemen of Virginia will send us a Dozen of their Sons, we will take great Care of their Education, instruct them in all we know, and make Men of them.

• • •

HIGH PLACES

An admirer once asked Winston Churchill, "Doesn't it thrill you to know that every time you make a speech the hall is packed to overflowing?"

Churchill replied, "It is quite flattering, but whenever I feel this way I always remember that if instead of making a political speech I was being hanged, the crowd would be twice as big."

• • •

HUNG JURY

In *Don Quixote*, Cervantes tells of a bridge at one end of which stand a gallows and a tribunal charged with enforcing this law:

> If anyone crosses by this bridge from one side to the other he shall declare on oath where he is going to and with

what object; and if he swears truly, he shall be allowed to pass, but if falsely, he shall be put to death for it by hanging on the gallows erected there, without any remission.

The tribunal allows many travelers to pass freely, as it is easy to see that their declarations are truthful. But one day a man appears who swears that he has come expressly to die upon the gallows.

"It is asked of your worship, *señor* governor, what are the judges to do with this man?"

• • •

A THANKFUL VILLAGE

The township of Thierville, in Normandy, has not lost any service personnel in France's last five wars—the Franco-Prussian war of 1870, either world war, the First Indochina War, or the Algerian War.

It was the only community in France in which no war memorial was erected between 1919 and 1925—the only one with no dead to mourn.

• • •

INTO THE FIRE

Fighter pilot William Rankin bailed out of a failing jet in 1959 and found himself inside a thunderstorm:

❝I saw lightning all around me in every shape imaginable. When very close, it appeared mainly as a huge, bluish sheet several feet thick, sometimes sticking close to me in pairs, like the blades of a scissors, and I had the distinct feeling that I was being sliced in two. It was raining so torrentially that I thought I would drown in midair. Several times I had held my breath, fearing that otherwise I might inhale quarts of water. How silly, I thought, they're going to find you hanging from some tree, in your parachute harness, your lungs filled with water, wondering how on earth you drowned.

The storm cloud toyed with him for 45 minutes before it finally put him down—65 miles from where he'd bailed out.

• • •

TRIBUTE

A letter from William James to his 8-year-old daughter Peggy, June 19, 1895:

Sweet Peg.

I am very happy here, and fear that you may already have gone up to Chocorua with your Mamma. Yesterday a beautiful humming bird came into the library and spent two hours without resting, trying to find his way out by the skylight in the ceiling. You never saw such untiring strength. Filled with pity for his fatigue, I went into the garden and culled a beautiful rose. The moment I held it up in my hand under the skylight, the angelic bird flew down into it and rested there as in a nest—the beautifullest sight you ever saw.

Your loving
Dad

• • •

NO CONNECTION

In 1816, enterprising meteorologist Francis Ronalds strung eight miles of wire through his London garden and created a working telegraph. When he offered it to the British Admiralty, he received this response:

    “ “Mr. Barrow presents his compliments to Mr. Ronalds, and acquaints him, with reference to his note of the 3rd inst., that telegraphs of any kind are now wholly unnecessary, and that no other than the one now in use [i.e., semaphore] will be adopted.

So Ronalds gave up. “I felt very little disappointment, and not a shadow of resentment, on the occasion, because every one knows that telegraphs have long been great bores at the Admiralty,” he wrote. “I claim no indulgence for mere chimeras and chimera framers, and I hope to escape the fate of being ranked in that unenviable class.”

• • •

THE LAST CENT

You and a friend are playing a game. Between you is a pile of 15 pennies. You'll take turns removing pennies from the pile—each of you, on his turn, can choose to remove 1, 2, or 3 pennies. The loser is the one who removes the last penny. You go first. How should you play?

(See Answers and Solutions)

• • •

SIGNS AND WONDERS

❝COLUMBIA, S.C., May 29.—Closely following the appearance of the hand of flame in the heavens above Ohio comes a story from Darlington County, in this State, of a flying serpent. Last Sunday evening, just before sunset, Miss Ida Davis and her two younger sisters were strolling through the woods, when they were suddenly startled by the appearance of a huge serpent moving through the air above them. The serpent was distant only two or three rods when they first beheld it, and was sailing through the air with a speed equal to that of a hawk or buzzard, but without any visible means of propulsion. Its movements in its flight resembled those of a snake, and it looked a formidable object as it wound its way along, being apparently about 15 feet in length. The girls stood amazed and followed it with their eyes until it was lost to view in the distance. The flying serpent was also seen by a number of people in other parts of the county early in the afternoon of the same day, and by those it is represented as emitting a hissing noise which could be distinctly heard.

—*New York Times*, May 30, 1888

PART FOUR

JONATHAN SWIFT, ASTEROIDS, *and* MONOPOLY

DREAM TIME

In 1898 J.W. Dunne was staying at a hotel in Sussex when he dreamed he was arguing with one of the waiters. He was claiming that it was 4:30 in the afternoon, and the waiter maintained it was 4:30 in the morning. "With the apparent illogicality peculiar to all dreams, I concluded that my watch must have stopped; and, on extracting that instrument from my waistcoat pocket, I saw, looking down on it, that this was precisely the case. It had stopped—with the hands at half-past four. With that I awoke."

He lit a match to see whether his watch really had stopped. It was not by his bedside, but after some hunting he found it lying on a chest of drawers. It had stopped, and the hands stood at 4:30. Noting the coincidence, he wound the watch and returned to bed.

On coming downstairs the next morning, he went to the nearest clock in order to restore the watch to the correct time. He expected to find it off by several hours, as he supposed it had stopped during the previous afternoon and was rewound in the middle of the night.

But "to my absolute amazement I found that the hands had lost only some two or three minutes, about the amount of time which had elapsed between my waking from the dream and rewinding the watch."

In other words, the dream watch and the waking watch had stopped at the same moment. Possibly the sleeping Dunne had sensed that his watch's familiar ticking had stopped, and this had informed his dream. "But—how did I come to see, in that dream, that the hands stood, as they actually did, at half-past four?"

• • •

ALIGNMENT

By Lee Sallows: Assign the letters JHMLCNVTURISEYAPO to
the integers -8 to 8 and you get:

```
S+U+N              =               3+0-3  = 0
M+E+R+C+U+R+Y  = -6+4+1-4+0+1+5  = 1
V+E+N+U+S          =          -2+4-3+0+3  = 2
E+A+R+T+H          =           4+6+1-1-7  = 3
M+A+R+S            =            -6+6+1+3  = 4
J+U+P+I+T+E+R  = -8+0+7+2-1+4+1  = 5
S+A+T+U+R+N        =        3+6-1+0+1-3  = 6
U+R+A+N+U+S        =        0+1+6-3+0+3  = 7
N+E+P+T+U+N+E  = -3+4+7-1+0-3+4  = 8
P+L+U+T+O          =           7-5+0-1+8  = 9
```

And ERIS gives 10.

• • •

AUTHORIAL DISTASTE

Kingsley Amis on Dylan Thomas, 1947: "I have got to the stage now with mr toss that I have only reached with Chaucer and Dryden, not even with Milton, that of VIOLENTLY WISHING that the man WERE IN FRONT OF ME, so that I could be DEMONIACALLY RUDE to him about his GONORRHEIC RUBBISH, and end up by WALKING ON HIS FACE and PUNCHING HIS PRIVY PARTS."

Mark Twain on Jane Austen, 1898: "Every time I read *Pride and Prejudice* I want to dig her up and hit her over the skull with her own shin-bone."

Byron on Keats, 1820: "No more Keats, I entreat: flay him alive; if some of you don't I must skin him myself: there is no bearing the driveling idiotism of the Mankin."

Virginia Woolf on D.H. Lawrence, 1932: "English has one million words: why confine yourself to six?"

Cyril Connolly on George Orwell, 1973: "He would not blow his nose without moralising on conditions in the handkerchief industry."

In reviewing Tom Wolfe's 742-page *A Man in Full* in the *New York Review of Books* in 1998, Norman Mailer wrote: "At certain points, reading the work can even be said to resemble the act of making love to a three-hundred-pound woman. Once she gets on top, it's all over. Fall in love, or be asphyxiated."

• • •

THE SOUL TRIAL

When Arizona copper prospector James Kidd disappeared in 1949, he left behind a curious will:

❝ this is my first and only will and is dated the second day in January 1946. I have no heirs have not married in my life, after all my funeral expenses have been paid and #100, one hundred dollars to some preacher of the gospital to say fare well at my grave sell all my property which is all in cash and stocks with E F Hutton Co Phoenix some in safety deposit box, and have this balance money go into a reserach or some scientific proof of a soul of the human body which leaves at death I think in time their can be a Photograph of soul leaving the human at death, James Kidd

He left it in a safe deposit box, so it didn't come to light until 1963, by which time Kidd's estate had appreciated to nearly $200,000. This attracted more than 100 claimants, each of which argued it was best qualified to find the human soul. The Neurological Sciences Foundation of Phoenix, for example, said that it was working with hallucinogenic agents, biochemical controls of the brain, and the nervous system. "To the extent that the 'soul' is a function of the human body," it insisted, "to this extent our work . . . is relevant to the intent of the will."

Arizona superior court judge Robert L. Myers finally awarded the legacy to a local neurological institute, but after an additional six years of litigation it went to the American Society for Psychical Research. "The Kidd legacy was not only a windfall," wrote Nicholas Wade in *Science*, "but proved the parapsychologists could at least convince a court of the seriousness of their intentions."

• • •

NEW YEAR BE DAMNED

Jonathan Swift's "Resolutions—When I Come to Be Old":

- Not to Marry a young Woman.
- Keep young Company unless they reely desire it.
- Be peevish or morose, or suspicious.
- Scorn present Ways, or Wits, or Fashions, or Men, or War, &c.
- Be fond of Children, or let them come near me hardly.
- Tell the same Story over and over to the same People.
- Be covetous.
- Neglect decency, or cleenlyness, for fear of falling into Nastyness.
- Be over severe with young People, but give Allowances for their youthfull follyes, and Weeknesses.
- Be influenced by, or give ear to knavish tatling Servants, or others.
- Be too free of advise nor trouble any but those that desire it.
- Desire some good Friends to inform me which of these Resolutions I break, or neglect, & wherein; and reform accordingly.
- Talk much, nor of my self.
- Boast of my former beauty, or strength, or favor with Ladyes, &c.
- Hearken to Flatteryes, nor conceive I can be beloved by a young woman.
- Be positive or opiniative.
- Sett up for observing all these Rules, for fear I should observe none.

• • •

PILLOW PROBLEM

From a 1921 essay by A.A. Milne:

❝ TERALBAY is not a word which one uses much in ordinary life. Rearrange the letters, however, and it becomes such a word. A friend—no, I can call him a friend no longer—a person gave me this collection of letters as I was going to bed and challenged me to make a proper word of it. He added that Lord Melbourne—this, he alleged, is a well-known historical fact—Lord Melbourne had given this word to Queen Victoria once, and it had kept her awake the whole night. After this, one could not be so disloyal as to solve it at once. For two hours or so, therefore, I merely toyed with it. Whenever I seemed to be getting warm I hurriedly thought of something else. This quixotic loyalty has been the undoing of me; my chances of a solution have slipped by, and I am beginning to fear that they will never return. While this is the case, the only word I can write about is TERALBAY.

The answer is not RATEABLY, or BAT-EARLY, which "ought to mean something, but it doesn't." Rudolf Flesch notes that TRAYABLE is not a word, and that, though TEARABLY appears in small type in Webster's Unabridged, "it obviously won't do."

What's the answer? There's no trick—it's an ordinary English word.

(See Answers and Solutions)

• • •

BALANCE

AMBIDEXTROUS is ambidextrous—its first half draws on the first half of the alphabet, its second on the second.

• • •

UNQUOTE

"The American who first discovered
Columbus made a bad discovery."

—G.C. Lichtenberg

• • •

SO ORDERED

On Feb. 18, 1986, frustrated that heavy rains had prevented some jurors from reaching his court, U.S. District Court Judge Samuel

King said, "I hereby order that it cease raining by Tuesday. Let's see how that works."

California immediately entered five years of severe drought, with strict water rationing.

When colleagues reminded King of his order in 1991, he said, "I hereby rescind my order of February 18, 1986, and order that rain shall fall in California beginning February 27, 1991." Later that day the state received 4 inches of rain, the heaviest storm in a decade, and two further storms added another 3 inches.

In a letter to a local newspaper, King said this was "proof positive that we are a nation governed by laws."

• • •

KING OF THE HILL

❝❝On Tuesday week, as the coal train on the Swannington line was proceeding to Leicester, and when near Glenfield, the engine-driver suddenly perceived a fine bullock appear on the line, and turn to meet the train, head to head with the engine. The animal ran directly up to its fiery antagonist, and by the contact was killed on the spot. There was no time to stop the train before the infuriated beast came up. It was afterwards discovered that the animal belonged to Mr. Hassell, of Glenfield, and made its way on to the line from the field adjoining.

—*Leicester Journal*, reprinted in the *Times*,
Aug. 10, 1849

• • •

CONSTELLATION

German astronomer Karl Reinmuth discovered and named more than 400 asteroids. Among them are these eight:

1227 Geranium
1228 Scabiosa
1229 Tilia
1230 Riceia
1231 Auricula
1232 Cortusa
1233 Kobresia
1234 Elyna

Their initials spell G. STRACKE, for Gustav Stracke, a fellow astronomer who had asked that no planet be named after him. In this way Reinmuth could honor his colleague without contradicting his wish.

• • •

A PENNY SAVED

Benjamin Franklin once wrote, "I have sometimes almost wished it had been my destiny to have been born two or three centuries hence." In one ingenious way he managed to touch the 20th century directly.

In 1785, French mathematician Charles-Joseph Mathon de la Cour wrote a parody of *Poor Richard's Almanac* in which the idealistic main character deposits a small amount of money to collect interest over several centuries, enabling him to fund valuable projects after his death. Franklin, who was 79 years old, thanked him for the idea and bequeathed £1,000 each to the cities of Boston and Philadelphia, stipulating that it gather interest for 200 years. When it came due in 1990, the Philadelphia fund had accumulated $2 million, which the city spent on scholarships for local high school students. The Boston trust amassed nearly $5 million, which went to establish the Benjamin Franklin Institute of Technology.

"What astonished me in reading his will was how much energy, intelligence and vigor came through after 200 years," lawyer Gerard J. St. John, who oversaw the distribution of the Philadelphia funds, told the *Philadelphia Inquirer*. "I began to have a greater appreciation for Franklin's place in history."

• • •

SOUL MATES

Lewis Carroll discerns a public danger in birthday toasts, from a letter to Gertrude Chataway, Oct. 13, 1875:

❝I am very much afraid, next time Sybil looks for you, she'll find you sitting by the sad sea-wave, and crying 'Boo! hoo! Here's Mr. Dodgson has drunk my health, and I haven't got any left!' And how it will puzzle Dr. Maund, when he is sent for to see you! 'My dear Madam, I'm very sorry to say your little girl has got no health at all! I never saw such a thing in my life!' 'Oh, I can easily explain it!' your mother will say. 'You see she would go and make friends with a strange gentleman, and yesterday he drank her health!' 'Well, Mrs. Chataway,' he will say, 'the only way to cure her is to wait till his next birthday, and then for her to drink his health.'

"And then we shall have changed healths. I wonder how

you'll like mine! Oh, Gertrude, I wish you wouldn't talk such nonsense!"

• • •

STRIDE RIGHT

A mother takes two strides to her daughter's three. If they set out walking together, each starting with the right foot, when will they first step together with the left?

(See Answers and Solutions)

• • •

SO IT GOES

❝ The Man who thought about Proteids sat by the roadside, writing with an indelible pencil in a little notebook. And Spring, all in pink and white, came tripping by, and cried to him: 'I will dance for you! Watch me dance!' She danced very prettily, but the Man went on writing, and never looked at her once. So Spring, being young, burst into tears, and told her sister, Summer.

Summer said to herself: 'Spring is very foolish to cry. Probably he does not like dancing. I will sing to him.' She sang a beautiful sleepy song to him, but he never listened, being busy writing in his little notebook. Summer was indignant, and told her sister, Autumn.

Autumn said: 'There are many good men who do not like dancing. I will give him some of my wine.' So she went to the Man and offered him her purple wine, but he merely said, 'I do not drink wine,' and resumed his writing. Then Autumn was very angry indeed, and told her big brother, Winter, all that had passed.

Winter was an enormous fellow, with a dreadful roar and howl, and every time he moved, snowflakes came whirling from his flowing robes. 'Show me the fellow,' he bellowed, puffing out his cheeks. Then he saw the Man who thought about Proteids, still sitting by the roadside.

'Do you know me?' roared Winter, and the Man looked and his teeth chattered like dead men's bones.

Then Winter seized him by the neck and whirled him round and round, and finally flung him over his left shoulder into space.

And the Man who thought about Proteids has not been seen since, but, the other day, a boy found the little note-book lying by the roadside.

—J.B. Priestley, *Brief Diversions*, 1922

• • •

HELLO GOODBYE

In 1902, disgusted with the "characteristic American custom of promiscuous, unsought and unauthorized introductions," Ambrose Bierce proposed a new social convention—disintroductions:

❝ Mr. White—Mr. Black, knowing the low esteem in which you hold each other, I have the honor to disintroduce you from Mr. Green.

Mr. Black (bowing)—Sir, I have long desired the advantage of your unacquaintance.

Mr. Green (bowing)—Charmed to unmeet you, sir. Our acquaintance (the work of a most inconsiderate and unworthy person) has distressed me beyond expression. We are greatly indebted to our good friend here for his tact in repairing the mischance.

Mr. White—Thank you. I'm sure you will become very good strangers.

"This is only the ghost of a suggestion," Bierce wrote. "Of course the plan is capable of an infinite elaboration. Its capital defect is that the persons who are now so liberal with their unwelcome introductions, will be equally lavish with their disintroductions, and will estrange the best of friends with as little ceremony as they now observe in their more fiendish work."

• • •

REQUIRED READING

In 1990, Spanish philosopher Jon Perez Laraudogoitia submitted an article to *Mind* entitled "This Article Should Not Be Rejected by *Mind*." In it, he argued:

1. If statement 1 in this argument is trivially true, then this article should be accepted.
2. If statement 1 were false, then its antecedent ("statement 1 in this argument is trivially true") would be true, which means that statement 1 itself would be true, a contradiction. So statement 1 must be true.

3. But that seems wrong, since *Mind* is a serious journal and shouldn't publish trivial truths.

4. That means statement 1 must be either false or a non-trivial truth. We know it can't be false (#2), so it must be a non-trivial truth, and its antecedent ("statement 1 in this argument is trivially true") is false.

5. What then is the truth value of its consequent, "this article should be accepted"? If this were false then *Mind* shouldn't publish the article; that can't be right, since the article consists of a non-trivial truth and its justification.

6. So the consequent must be true, and *Mind* should publish the article.

They published it. "This is, I believe, the first article in the whole history of philosophy the content of which is concerned exclusively with its own self, or, in other words, which is totally self-referential," Laraudogoitia wrote. "The reason why it is published is because in it there is a proof that it should not be rejected and that is all."

• • •

GET OUT OF JAIL FREE

In 1941, as the British War Office searched for ways to help Allied prisoners escape from German POW camps, it found an unlikely partner: John Waddington Ltd., the U.K. licensee for *Monopoly.* "Games and pastimes" was an approved category of item to be included in care packages sent to captured soldiers, so Waddington's set about creating special sets to be sent to the camps.

Under the paper surface of each doctored board was a map printed on durable silk showing "escape routes from the particular prison to which each game was sent," Waddington's chairman Victor Watson told the Associated Press in 1985. "Into the other side of the board was inserted a tiny compass and several fine-quality files." Real French, German, and Italian currency was hidden in the stacks of *Monopoly* money.

MI-9, the intelligence division charged with helping POWs escape, smuggled the games into prison camps, where prisoners would remove the aids and then destroy the sets in order to prevent their captors from divining the scheme.

"It is not known how many airmen escaped thanks to these *Monopoly* games," writes Philip Orbanes in *The Game Makers*, his 2004 history of Parker Brothers, "but 35,000 POWs did break out of prison camps and reach partisans who helped them to safety."

• • •

OPPOSITES EXACT

Prove that, at any given moment, there are two points on the equator that are diametrically opposed yet have the same temperature.

(See Answers and Solutions)

• • •

OVER AND OUT

If it's a sin to end a sentence with one preposition, then presumably it's even worse to end it with two. How far can we take this? For the August 1968 issue of *Word Ways: The Journal of Recreational Linguistics*, Darryl Francis devised one sentence that ends with nine prepositions. If the Yardbirds' 1966 single "Over, Under, Sideways, Down" were exported to Australia and then retrieved by a traveler, the question might be asked:

"What did he bring 'Over, Under, Sideways, Down' up from Down Under for?"

Inspired, Ralph Beaman pointed out that if this issue of the journal were now brought to a boy who slept on the upper floor of a lighthouse, he might ask:

"What did you bring me the magazine I didn't want to be read to out of about '"Over Under, Sideways, Down" up from Down Under' up around for?"

"This has a total of fifteen terminal prepositions," writes Ross Eckler, "but the end is not in sight; for now the little boy can complain in similar vein about the reading material provided in this issue of *Word Ways*, adding a second 'to out of about' at the beginning and 'up around for' at the end of the preposition string. The mind boggles at the infinite regress which has now been established."

• • •

SOLITAIRE

In 1985, 61-year-old Oreste Lodi came up with a novel way to raid his own trust fund: He sued himself. In a suit filed in the Shasta County (Calif.) Superior Court, Lodi named himself as defendant, failed to answer the complaint, then asked that a default judgment be entered against himself.

When a judge threw out the case, he appealed to the Third Appellate District, filing briefs on both sides. Unfortunately, the appeals court called Lodi's case "a slam-dunk frivolous complaint."

"This result cannot be unfair to Mr. Lodi," it noted. "Although it is true that, as plaintiff and appellant, he loses, it is equally true that, as defendant and respondent, he wins! It is hard to imagine a more evenhanded application of justice."

• • •

ID BY WOOLWORTH

In 1938, a wallet manufacturer in Lockport, N.Y., decided to include sample Social Security cards in its products. The company's vice president thought it would be clever to use the actual Social Security number of his secretary, Hilda Whitcher.

It wasn't. The sample card was half-size, printed in red, and bore the word SPECIMEN in large letters, but by 1943 more than 5,000 people were using Whitcher's number as their own. The Social Security Administration voided the card and started a publicity campaign to educate users, but over the years more than 40,000 people reported the number as their own, some as recently as 1977.

"They started using the number," Whitcher marveled. "They thought it was their own. I can't understand how people can be so stupid. I can't understand that."

• • •

"A HORSE FOUND SWIMMING IN THE OCEAN"

❝❝Capt. Edwards, of the fishing smack *Amelia*, reports that when off 'Skunnett,' on the Rhode Island shore, some time since, he discovered an object swimming off his bow which he finally made out to be a horse. He made sail but could not overhaul the animal, which was making desperate struggles to reach the main land three miles away. At times he would disappear from sight in the waves which broke over him,—the sea running very high at the time,—but a moment later would reappear, and with a loud snort and toss of the head, would shake off the water from his ears and eyes, and then renew the struggle. At last he made the shore, and, without pausing a moment, dashed up the beach, his long tail and curling mane floating outward on the wind. The splendid animal was possessed of immense strength, else he could not have swam that long distance in such a sea. Where he came from nobody knows. No vessel was in sight from which he could have escaped.

—James Baird McClure, ed., *Entertaining Anecdotes From Every Available Source*, 1879

• • •

IN A WORD

cultrivorous
adj. devouring knives

lychnobite
n. one who works at night and sleeps during the day

eriff
n. a two-year-old canary

omnilegent
adj. having read everything

• • •

RUBBING SHOULDERS

Every number greater than 8 has at least two letters in common with each of its neighbors.

• • •

HOPE AND CHANGE

❝One dollar and eighty-seven cents. That was all. And sixty cents of it was in pennies. Pennies saved one and two at a time by bulldozing the grocer and the vegetable man and the butcher until one's cheeks burned with the silent imputation of parsimony that such close dealing implied. Three times Della counted it. One dollar and eighty-seven cents. And the next day would be Christmas.

That's the first paragraph of "The Gift of the Magi." Does it contain a blunder? If Della has $1.87, and pennies make up 60 cents of it, what constitutes the remaining $1.27?

There are two possibilities. The story doesn't say that only 60 cents of the total was in pennies; possibly 62 cents was, though this makes Della's observation seem pointless. The second possibility is that the story is set in the late 19th century, when the United States was still minting two- and three-cent pieces—though there's no other indication that this is the case.

So is this a blunder? Only O. Henry knows for sure.

• • •

AMUSED

In 1878 Queen Victoria invited to lunch an elderly naval officer who was hard of hearing. For a time the two discussed the recent sinking of the naval training ship *Eurydice*. Then, to turn to a lighter subject, the queen inquired after the admiral's sister.

"Well, ma'am," he replied, "I am going to have her turned over and take a good look at her bottom and have it well scraped."

"The effect of his answer was stupendous," wrote the queen's grandson, Kaiser Wilhelm II. "My grandmother put down her knife and fork, hid her face in her handkerchief and shook and heaved with laughter till the tears rolled down her face."

• • •

GARISH

On a trip to America, G.K. Chesterton was taken one night to see the lights of Broadway.

"What a glorious garden of wonders this would be," he said, "to any one who was lucky enough to be unable to read."

• • •

COMING TO AMERICA

❝It is a hard and lengthy task to become acquainted with the vagaries of the language, not to mention the forgotten or altered meanings of many words. Some of these vagaries are aptly illustrated by the story of the Frenchman who said to an American:

I am going to leave my hotel. I paid my bill yesterday, and I said to the landlord, 'Do I owe anything else?' He said, 'You are square.' 'What am I?' He said again, 'You are square.' 'That's strange,' said I. 'I lived so long that I never knew I was square before.' Then, as I was going away, he shook me by the hand, saying, 'I hope you'll be round soon.' I said, 'I thought you said I was square; now you hope I'll be round.' He laughed and said, 'When I tell you you'll be round, I mean you won't be long.' Then, seeing me count my change twice over, he said, 'Are you short?' I did not know how many forms he wished me to assume: however, I was glad he did not call me flat.

—William S. Bridge, "The English Language," in
The Typographical Journal, March 15, 1902

• • •

HEY!

If Martians are observing us, how can we show them we're intelligent?

Carl Friedrich Gauss proposed marking a huge right triangle on the Siberian plain; Austrian astronomer Joseph von Littrow suggested carving a perfect circle in the Sahara and filling it with burning kerosene.

Joseph Pulitzer favored a more direct approach: He wanted to build a huge billboard in New Jersey recommending his newspaper to inquiring Martians.

He pressed the idea until an assistant asked, "What language shall we print it in?"

• • •

PEST CONTROL

This looks a bit. . . *direct*, but it dates from 1882. James Williams needed a device that would destroy a burrowing animal and give an alarm so that it could be reset. His solution was a revolver attached to a treadle. Touché.

The patent abstract adds, "This invention may also be used in connection with a door or window, so as to kill any person or thing opening the door or window to which it is attached." Evidently Williams had bigger problems than rodents.

• • •

ILLUMINATION

In 1969, as NASA was preparing to send the first men to the moon, it invited world leaders to compose goodwill messages to be recorded on a silicon disc and left on the Sea of Tranquility.

Most of them sent rather banal greetings, but Félix Houphouët-Boigny, president of Ivory Coast, sent this:

> ❝At the moment when man's oldest dream is becoming a reality, I am very thankful for NASA's kind attention in offering me the services of the first human messenger to set foot on the Moon and carry the words of the Ivory Coast. I would hope that when this passenger from the sky leaves man's imprint on lunar soil, he will feel how proud we are to belong to the generation which has accomplished this feat.
>
> I hope also that he would tell the Moon how beautiful it is when it illuminates the nights of the Ivory Coast. I especially wish that he would turn towards our planet Earth and cry out how insignificant the problems which torture men are, when viewed from up there.

PART FIVE

LIFE, NANCY DREW, *and* THE NOBEL PRIZE

SILVERTON BOBBIE

In 1923, the Brazier family traveled from Oregon to Indiana, bringing their 2-year-old collie/shepherd mix, Bobbie. They were separated in Wolcott, Ind., when Bobbie was chased off by a group of local dogs, and after three weeks the family reluctantly returned to Oregon.

Exactly six months later, the family's youngest daughter was walking down a Silverton street when she recognized a bedraggled dog. At her voice he "fairly flew at Nova, leaping up again and again to cover her face with kisses and making half-strangled, sobbing sounds of relief and delight as if he could hardly voice his wordless joy."

He had traveled more than 2,800 miles. He was identified by three scars, and by letters the family later received from people who had housed and fed him along the way. The "wonder dog" received national publicity, and well-wishers gave him a jewel-studded harness, a silver collar, keys to various cities, and "a miniature bungalow, which weighed about nine hundred pounds, with eight windows curtained with silk." He died in 1927, and Rin Tin Tin laid a wreath on his grave.

• • •

DOMESTIC HARMONY

The *Musical World* of London, Nov. 28, 1874, reports a surprising project—apparently a Massachusetts composer set the entire American constitution to music:

❝The authors of the Constitution of the Union thought

more of reason than of rhyme, and their prose is not too well adapted to harmony, but the patriotic inspiration of Mr. Greeler, the Boston composer, overcomes every difficulty. He has made his score a genuine musical epopœia, and had it performed before a numerous public. The performance did not last less than six hours. The preamble of the Constitution forms a broad and majestic recitative, well sustained by altos and double basses. The first clause is written for a tenor; the other choruses are given to the bass, soprano, and baritone. The music of the clause treating of state's rights is written in a minor key for bass and tenor. At the end of every clause, the recitative of the preamble is re-introduced and then repeated by the chorus. The constitutional amendments are treated as fugues and serve to introduce a formidable finale, in which the big drum and the gong play an important part. The general instrumentation is very scholarly, and the harmony surprising.

The music has been lost, but it would be out of date now anyway—we've added 12 amendments since then.

• • •

RETURN TO SENDER

On Sept. 30, 1826, a beachcomber found a bottle in the surf at Barbados. Inside was a penciled note:

❝ The ship the *Kent*, Indiaman, is on fire. Elizabeth, Joanna, and myself commit our spirits into the hands of our blessed Redeemer; His grace enables us to be quite composed in the awful prospect of entering eternity. Dun. McGregor. 1st of March, 1825. Bay of Biscay.

Strangely, the note's author arrived a short time later. Duncan MacGregor, now a lieutenant colonel in the 93rd Highlanders, had been a major bound for India when the *Kent* took fire. After he and his family had been rescued by a passing brig, an explosion aboard the burning vessel had cast the bottle into the sea, and it had floated across the Atlantic as if to rejoin him.

A regimental historian confirmed the story after MacGregor's death in 1881. "[The note] is still preserved by his son, who was at the time of the loss of the *Kent* a child of only five weeks old, and was the first saved from the wreck."

• • •

EXERCISES

One summer afternoon in 1917, Royal Flying Corps trainee Graham Donald prepared to try a new maneuver with his Sopwith Camel. He ascended into a vertical loop, intending to flip the plane at the top and fly off in the opposite direction. Unfortunately, when the airplane was fully inverted at 6,000 feet, his safety belt gave way and "suddenly I dived clean through it and fell out of the cockpit."

"The first 2,000 feet passed very quickly, and terra firma looked damnably 'firma,'" he recalled later. But as he fell, "I began to hear my faithful little Camel somewhere nearby." He dropped onto the diving plane and managed to grip its top wing, "and that saved me from slithering straight through the propeller, which was glistening beautifully in the evening sunshine."

As the ground neared at 140 mph, he reached into the cockpit and pulled back on the control stick. Unfortunately, this sent the plane into an inverted spin. With 2,500 feet left, Donald managed to put his right foot on the stick and push it forward, and he found himself clinging to a plane that was flying upside down. He reached the controls, righted the plane, and climbed into the cockpit with about 800 feet to spare. To prevent further strain on the wings, he cut the engine and glided back to the airfield.

"I made an unusually good landing, but there was no one there to applaud—every man-jack of the squadron had mysteriously disappeared. After a minute or so, heads began to appear all over the place—popping up like bunny rabbits from every hole. Apparently, when I had pressed my foot on the control stick, I'd also pressed both triggers and the entire airfield had been sprinkled with bullets. Very wisely, the ground crew dived as one man for the nearest ditch."

• • •

SPIN CONTROL

We're playing Russian roulette. The revolver has six chambers, all empty. I put bullets in two adjacent chambers, spin the cylinder, hold the gun to my head, and pull the trigger. It clicks. Now it's your turn. Before pulling the trigger, you can choose to spin the cylinder again or leave it as it is. Which is better?

(See Answers and Solutions)

• • •

SURFACE MATTERS

If you touch a gold ball, you touch its surface and you touch gold. It seems reasonable to conclude that the surface is made of gold. But University of Exeter computer scientist Antony Galton points out that the surface is two-dimensional; it can't contain any quantity of gold.

What then is it? We can't say it's the outermost layer of gold atoms, for that's a film with two surfaces. And we can't say it's an abstract boundary with no physical existence, for we can see it and touch it. So what is it?

J.L. Austin asked, "Where and what exactly is the surface of a cat?"

• • •

SIBLING RIVALRY

"Supposing some unfortunate lady was confined with twins and one child was born 10 minutes before 1 o'clock; if the clock was put back, the registration of the time of birth of the two children would be reversed. . . . Such an alteration might conceivably affect the property and titles in that house."—Lord Balfour of Burleigh, opposing daylight saving time, House of Lords, May 1916

• • •

UNQUOTE

"History is philosophy teaching by examples."—Thucydides

• • •

REPEAT PERFORMANCE

The index of the 57th edition of the *Handbook of Chemistry and Physics* includes the entry *Sea water, see Water, sea.*

The Latin phrase *Malo malo malo malo* can be translated as "I would rather be in an apple tree than a bad boy in adversity."

Betty and Jock Leslie-Melville's 1973 book *Elephant Have Right of Way* cites the Swahili sentence *Wale wa Liwali wale wale* ("the people of the Arab chieftain eat cooked rice"). "How is it pronounced? Just say 'Wally' five times."

And in Finnish the utterance "Kokko, gather up the whole bonfire. The whole bonfire? The whole bonfire, Kokko, gather up!" is rendered as *Kokko, kokoa koko kokko kokoon. Koko kokko? Koko kokko, Kokko, kokoa kokoon!*

• • •

IN A WORD

hallelujatic
adj. containing hallelujahs

apricity
n. the warmth of the sun in winter

andabatarian
adj. struggling while blindfolded

bemute
v. to drop dung on from above

• • •

DIY

On a voyage to England in 1757, Ben Franklin narrowly escaped shipwreck.

Afterward, he wrote to his wife, "The bell ringing for church, we went thither immediately, and with hearts full of gratitude, returned sincere thanks to God for the mercies we had received.

"Were I a Roman Catholic, perhaps I should on this occasion vow to build a chapel to some saint, but as I am not, if I were to vow at all, it should be to build a light-house."

• • •

SYMPATHY

66A most singular circumstance has recently occurred in Louisville. One Robert Sadler being arraigned on a writ of *lunatico inquirendo,* the following appeared in testimony: It was alleged that in the night time he would alarm his family and his neighbors with screams as if in severe pain, exclaiming that he felt the pain inflicted upon persons at a distance, by amputation or other causes. Mr. Sadler was said to be of good character and incapable of wilfully feigning what he did not feel, and therefore was supposed by his friends to be insane. In consequence of this belief a writ was issued to make the proper legal inquiry and to decide the question. The jury however could not agree to call him insane and he was discharged. It was proved that he uttered his cries and expressions of pain at the precise time that those with whose sufferings he claimed to be in sympathy, were actually undergoing the operations, which would cause similar pain; and this under circumstances which precluded the belief that he could have been aware, by external means, of the time or place at which such operations were to take place. The length of time during which he had displayed this morbid sensibility had been so prolonged, that if he had really been practicing a deception it could scarcely have failed to be discovered. In his conversation, and in all other particulars except the one we have described, Mr. Sadler gave no evidence of anything except the most perfect sanity. The case seems to be well authenticated, and if the truth of the details can be relied upon is altogether a very remarkable one.

—*Scientific American*, Dec. 16, 1868

• • •

UPSTAIRS DOWNSTAIRS

When Richard Feynman won the Nobel Prize in 1965, CERN director Victor Weisskopf worried that he would be driven out of physics and into administration. He goaded Feynman into signing a wager before witnesses:

> ❝Mr. FEYNMAN will pay the sum of TEN DOLLARS to Mr. WEISSKOPF if at any time during the next TEN YEARS (i.e. before the THIRTY FIRST DAY OF DECEMBER of the YEAR ONE THOUSAND NINE HUNDRED AND SEVENTY FIVE), the said MR. FEYNMAN has held a 'responsible position.'

The two agreed: "For the purpose of the aforementioned WAGER, the term 'responsible position' shall be taken to signify a position which, by reason of its nature, compels the holder to issue instructions to other persons to carry out certain acts, notwithstanding the fact that the holder has no understanding whatsoever of that which he is instructing the aforesaid persons to accomplish."

Feynman, who once called administration an "occupational disease," collected the $10 in 1976.

• • •

THE L-8 MYSTERY

At 6:03 on the morning of Aug. 16, 1942, U.S. Navy blimp *L-8* ascended from Treasure Island in San Francisco Bay to conduct an anti-submarine patrol along the coast of California. Aboard were pilot Ernest Cody and ensign Charles Adams. The flight proceeded uneventfully until 7:42, when Cody reported that they'd spotted an oil slick and were going to investigate.

At 11:15, caddies at a seaside golf club saw the airship float in from the sea, its motors silent. Descending, it struck some telephone lines and the roofs of several homes before coming to rest in Daly City. The first person to reach the downed ship, volunteer fireman William Morris, was surprised at what he found: "The doors were open and nobody was in the cabin."

There was no trace of Cody or Adams. Though most of the fuel had been dumped, the parachutes and life raft were stored appropriately, and the radio was in working order. Only the crew were missing.

After a search, the Navy declared itself certain that "the men were NOT in the ship at any time it traveled over land." Two fishing vessels near the oil slick testified that they'd seen the blimp descend to investigate, but nothing had fallen or dropped from it.

That's all. A Coast Guard search found nothing. Cody and Adams were both declared missing, then pronounced dead a year later. No one knows what became of them.

• • •

WHO'S COUNTING?

In the 14th century, an unnamed Kabbalistic scholar declared that the universe contains 301,655,722 angels.

In 1939, English astrophysicist Sir Arthur Eddington calculated that it contains 15,747,724,136,275,002,577,605,653,961,181, 555,468,044,717,914,527,116,709,366,231,425,076,185,631,031,296 electrons. "Some like to understand what they believe in," wrote Stanislaw Lec. "Others like to believe in what they understand."

• • •

SWINE WAVE

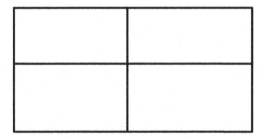

A bewildering puzzle by Lewis Carroll: Place 24 pigs in these sties so that, no matter how many times one circles the sties, he always find that the number in each sty is closer to 10 than the number in the previous one.

(See Answers and Solutions)

• • •

SELF-CONTRADICTING WORDS

Words whose meanings contradict one another:

BILL ("monetary note" and "statement of debt")

BUCKLE ("to secure" and "to collapse")
CLEAVE ("to separate" and "to bring together")
DOWNHILL ("progressively easier" and "progressively worse")
DUST ("to add dust" and "to remove dust")
FAST ("quick-moving" and "immobile")
GARNISH ("to add to" and "to take from")
MODEL ("archetype" and "copy")
OVERSIGHT ("attention" and "inattention")
PEER ("noble" and "person of equal rank")
PUZZLE ("to pose a problem" and "to try to solve a problem")
SANCTION ("to permit" and "to restrict")

And TABLE means both "to present for consideration" and "to remove from consideration."

• • •

THE ST. ALBANS RAID

In October 1864, a score of young men drifted into St. Albans, a little Vermont town just south of the Canadian border. They arrived in small groups by train and coach, took rooms in local hotels, and began to pass time around town, observing the daily routines of the citizens.

On October 19, they held up three local banks simultaneously. There they revealed themselves to be Confederate soldiers, and as they collected the money they required the bank officers to take an oath of fealty to the South. Then they made off across the border. "They must have either had a guide who was acquainted with the road or had made a personal examination," wrote one investigator, "because there were places in the road where strangers would have gone the wrong way, but they made no mistake."

In all, the raiders made off with $208,000, about $3.2 million in today's dollars. They were apprehended, but the Canadian authorities refused to extradite them, and their leader, Bennett Young, traveled in Europe until it was safe to return to Kentucky after the war. His exploit became the northernmost land action in the Civil War.

• • •

THE KNEE ON ITS OWN

A lone knee wanders through the world,
A knee and nothing more;
It's not a tent, it's not a tree,
A knee and nothing more.

In battle once there was a man
Shot foully through and through;
The knee alone remained unhurt
As saints are said to do.

Since then it's wandered through the world,
A knee and nothing more.
It's not a tent, it's not a tree,
A knee and nothing more.

—Christian Morgenstern, 1905

• • •

SIGHS AND WHISPERS

Frustrated with the intertitles in silent films, Charles Pidgin invented a better solution in 1917: The performers would inflate balloons on which their dialogue was printed. "The blowing or inflation of the devices by the various characters of a photo-play will add to the realism of the picture by the words appearing to come from the mouth of the players," Pidgin wrote. Even better, "the size of the speech may be increased with the increase of various emotions depicted on the screen."

It's not too late to implement this.

• • •

PARTING ORDERS

Marshal Ney directed his own execution. The military commander, whom Napoleon had called "the bravest of the brave," was convicted of treason and executed by firing squad in December 1815. He refused a blindfold and requested the right to give the order to fire, which was granted:

"Soldiers, when I give the command to fire, fire straight at my heart. Wait for the order. It will be my last to you. I protest against my condemnation. I have fought a hundred battles for France, and not one against her . . . Soldiers, fire!"

Related: In 1849 Fyodor Dostoyevsky was arrested for his membership in a secret society of St. Petersburg intellectuals. He and his friends were standing before a firing squad when word came that the tsar had commuted their sentence. He spent the next four years at hard labor in Siberia.

• • •

CONTENDING IN VAIN

In December 2005, tired of endless credit-card offers, West Hollywood realtor Gary More scrawled NEVER WASTE A TREE across one application and mailed it in.

Chase Visa issued a card to "Never Waste Tree."

He cut it up.

• • •

MENU TROUBLE

Charles Ollier observed that GHOTI can be pronounced "fish":

- GH as in *laugh*
- O as in *women*
- TI as in *nation*

Melville Dewey, who devised the Dewey Decimal System, suggested that GHEAUGHTEIGHPTOUGH spells "potato":

- GH as in *hiccough*
- EAU as in *beau*
- GHT as in *naught*
- EIGH as in *neigh*
- PT as in *pterodactyl*
- OUGH as in *though*

This sort of thing can get out of hand quickly. In his 1845 *Plea for Phonotypy and Phonography*, Alexander John Ellis offered SCHIESOURRHCE for "scissors," PHAIGHPHEAW-RAIBT for "neither," PHAIGHPHEAWRAIBT for "favorite," PSOURRPHUAKNTW for "servant," and (fittingly) EOLOT-THOWGHRHOIGHUAY for "orthography."

GHOTI might even be silent:

- GH as in *though*
- O as in *people*
- T as in *ballet*
- I as in *business*

Other languages, it seems, have simply surrendered—the Klingon word for fish is *ghotI*.

• • •

OVERDUE

On Feb. 11, 1979, 27-year-old Scott Moorman and four friends set out from Hana, Maui, for a daylong fishing expedition aboard the *Sarah Joe*, a 16.5-foot fiberglass motorboat. They did not return. The Coast Guard searched for five days, and private searches continued much longer, but no trace of them was found. Nine and a half years later, in 1988, marine biologist John Naughton discovered a wrecked boat with Hawaiian registry on Taongi, the northernmost coral atoll in the Marshall Islands, 2,300 miles west of Hawaii. It was the *Sarah Joe*, and nearby, under a pile of stones and a driftwood cross, were the bones of Scott Moorman. How he came there, who buried him, and what became of the others remain unknown.

• • •

BUSINESS TRIP

As a joke, Michael Collins submitted a travel voucher for his trip aboard Gemini 10. NASA reimbursed him $8 per day, a total of $24.

In his autobiography, Collins notes that he could instead have claimed 7 cents a mile, which would have yielded $80,000.

But one of the original Mercury astronauts had already tried this—and had received a bill for "a couple of million dollars" for the rocket he'd used.

• • •

INSPIRATION

John Dryden agreed to serve as judge in an impromptu poetry competition among a group of friends, including the Duke of Buckingham, the Earl of Rochester, and Lord Dorset.

All the contestants worked thoughtfully at their entries except for Lord Dorset, who wrote two or three lines and passed them to Dryden almost immediately.

When everyone had finished, Dryden reviewed their submissions, and he smiled when he reached Dorset's. "I must acknowledge," he said, "that there are abundance of fine things in my hands, and such as do honor to the personages who wrote them, but I am under the indispensable necessity of giving the highest preference to Lord Dorset. I must request you will hear it yourselves, gentlemen, and I believe each and every one of you will approve my judgment:

I promise to pay John Dryden,
or order on demand,
the sum of five hundred pounds.
Dorset.

"I must confess that I am equally charmed with the style and the subject," Dryden said. "This kind of writing exceeds any other, whether ancient or modern."

•   •   •

APPLIED CHEMISTRY

When Hitler's army marched into Copenhagen, Niels Bohr had to decide how to safeguard the Nobel medals of James Franck and Max von Laue, which they had entrusted to him. Sending gold out of the country was almost a capital offense, and the physicists' names were engraved on the medals, making such an attempt doubly risky. Burying the medals seemed uncertain as well. Finally his friend the Hungarian physicist Georg von Hevesy invented a novel solution: He dissolved the medals in a jar of aqua regia, which Bohr left on a shelf in his laboratory while he fled to Sweden.

When he returned in 1945, the jar was still there. Bohr had

the gold recovered, and the Nobel Foundation recast it into two medals.

Chemist Hermann Mark found a way to escape Germany with his money: He used it to buy platinum wire, which he fashioned into coat hangers. Once he had brought these successfully through customs, he sold them to recover the money.

• • •

THE PIMLICO MYSTERY

On Dec. 28, 1885, London grocer Edwin Bartlett was discovered dead in his bed. In his stomach was a fatal quantity of chloroform, but, strangely, his throat and larynx showed no signs of the burning that liquid chloroform should have caused.

Bartlett's wife, Adelaide, was having an open romance with George Dyson, a local minister. It transpired that she had induced him to buy chloroform at local pharmacies in quantities too small to provoke suspicion, ostensibly to help treat Edwin, who was undergoing painful dental surgeries.

At trial, Adelaide's defense was simply that she had no way to get the chloroform into Edwin's stomach without passing it down his throat. The jury let her go.

"Now that Mrs. Bartlett has been acquitted," remarked pathologist Sir James Paget afterward, "she should tell us, in the interests of science, how she did it." Adelaide made no response. The puzzle of Edwin's death has never been solved.

• • •

CARRY ON

Letter to the *Times*, Feb. 6, 1946:

Sir,

I have just written you a long letter.

On reading it over, I have thrown it into the waste paper basket.

Hoping this will meet with your approval,

I am, Sir,

Your obedient Servant,

A.D. Wintle

• • •

LOOPY

You can measure a circle's circumference by "unrolling" it along a line, like this:

But note that the smaller circle unrolls at the same time . . . and it gives the same length. Clearly we could do the same thing with circles of any size. Do all circles have the same circumference?

• • •

R.I.P.

In memory ov
John Smith, who met
wierlent death neer this spot
18 hundred and 40 too. He was shot
by his own pistill;
It was not one of the new kind,
but a old fashioned
brass barrel, and of such is the
Kingdom of heaven.

—Headboard, Sparta Diggings, Calif., quoted in Walter
Henry Howe, *Here Lies*, 1900

• • •

THE HANDICAP

Zachary challenges his brother Alexander to a 100-meter race. Alexander crosses the finish line when Zachary has covered only 97 meters.

The two agree to a second race, and this time Alexander starts 3 meters behind the starting line.

If both brothers run at the same speed as in the first race, who will win?

(See Answers and Solutions)

• • •

THE MEANING OF LIFE

Along with art and love, life is one of those bedeviling concepts that we really ought to have a definition for but don't. Philosophers tend to regard the question as too scientific, and scientists as too philosophical. Linus Pauling observed that it's easier to study the subject than to define it, and J.B.S. Haldane opined that "no definition will cover its infinite and self-contradictory variety."

Classical definitions of life typically refer to structural features, growth, reproduction, metabolism, motion against force, response to stimuli, evolvability, and information content and transfer. But definitions built on these elements are prone to exceptions. Fire grows, moves, metabolizes, reproduces, and responds to stimuli, but is "nonliving." So are free-market economies and the Internet, which evolve, store representations of themselves, and behave "purposefully." I am nonreproducing but, I hope, still alive.

If we we look around us, it's hard to find a property that's unique to life, and even if we could, our observations are limited to Earth's biosphere, a tiny, tenuous environment like a film of water on a basketball. But if we expand our list to include abstract properties such as resistance to entropy, then we risk including alien phenomena that we might not regard intuitively as living.

Perhaps the answer is more poetic. "As I see it, the great and distinguishing feature of living things . . . is that they have needs—continual, and, incidentally, complex needs," wrote botanist Donald C. Peattie in 1935. "I cannot conceive how even so organized a dead system as a crystal can be said to need anything. But a living creature, even when it sinks into that half-death of hibernation, even the seed in the bottom of the driest Mongolian marsh, awaiting rain through two thousand years, still has needs while there is life in it."

• • •

THE PARADOX OF THE DIVIDED STICK

Take a whole stick and cut it in half. Half a minute later, cut each half in half. A quarter of a minute after that, cut each quarter in half, and so on *ad infinitum*. What will remain at the end of a minute? An infinite number of infinitely thin pieces? In his 1990 book *The Infinite*, Oxford philosopher A.W. Moore asks, "Do we so much as understand this?"

Does each piece have any width? If so, couldn't we reassemble them to form an infinitely long stick? If not, how can we assemble them to form anything at all?

• • •

THE BOOK FACTORY

The Hardy Boys, Nancy Drew, the Bobbsey Twins, and Tom Swift were all the product of one man, Edward Stratemeyer, a New Jersey author who wrote more than 1,300 books and eventually founded a syndicate of ghostwriters who pounded out juvenile mysteries based on his instructions.

Stratemeyer conceived the syndicate when his Rover Boys series proved so popular that he could not keep up with the demand for more books. He corralled a stable of hungry young writers, and in 1910 they were producing 10 new series annually. Each writer earned $50 to $250 for a manuscript he could produce in a month, working with characters and plot devised by Stratemeyer. Stratemeyer would review each completed manuscript for consistency and publish it under a pseudonym that he owned—Franklin W. Dixon, Carolyn Keene, Laura Lee Hope,

Victor Appleton. Each book in a series mentioned the thrilling earlier volumes and foreshadowed the next book. The formula worked so well that when Stratemeyer died in 1930 his daughter continued the business; when she died in 1982 the syndicate was selling more than 2 million books a year.

This sounds cynical, but it worked because Stratemeyer had a sympathetic understanding of what young readers wanted. "The trouble is that very few adults get next to the heart of a boy when choosing something for him to read," Stratemeyer wrote to a publisher in 1901. "A wide awake lad has no patience with that which is namby-pamby, or with that which he puts down as a 'study book' in disguise. He demands real flesh and blood heroes who do something."

PART SIX

ROSSINI, NEW ZEALAND, *and* TROMBONES

EXTRA

On Feb. 6, 1898, a worker preparing the front page of the *New York Times* added 1 to that day's issue number, 14,499, and got 15,000.

Amazingly, no one caught the error until 1999, when 24-year-old news assistant Aaron Donovan tallied the dates since the paper's founding in 1851 and found that the modern issue number was 500 too high. So on Jan. 1, 2000, the paper turned back the clock, reverting from 51,753 to 51,254.

"There is something that appeals to me about the way the issue number marks the passage of time across decades and centuries," Donovan wrote in a memo. "It has been steadily climbing for longer than anyone who has ever glanced at it has been alive. The 19th-century newsboy hawking papers in a snowy Union Square is in some minute way bound by the issue number to the Seattle advertising executive reading the paper with her feet propped up on the desk."

• • •

PUBLIC SERVANT

During the War of 1812, the Declaration of Independence hung in the office of Stephen Pleasonton, an auditor in the State Department. When word came that the British might march on Washington, Secretary of State James Monroe ordered Pleasonton to safeguard the department's important books and papers, so Pleasonton ordered linen bags made and began filling them with documents.

As he was doing this, Secretary of War John Armstrong Jr. passed through the building and remarked that the alarm was unnecessary; he did not believe that the British planned to attack the city.

"Had he followed the advice of the Secretary of War, an irreparable loss would have been sustained," noted the *New York Times* in 1905. "For the papers which Mr. Pleasonton had placed in the coarse linen bags comprised the secret journals of Congress, then not published; the correspondence of Gen. Washington, his commission resigned at the close of the war; the correspondence of Gen. Greene and other officers of the Revolution, a well as laws, treaties, and correspondence of the Department of State, from the adoption of the Constitution down to that time."

Pleasonton had the bags carted to a grist mill on the Virginia side of the Potomac. As he was leaving his office, he caught sight of the Declaration hanging on his wall. He took it down, cut it out of its frame, and carried it away with the other papers.

Feeling that even the grist mill was too vulnerable, Pleasonton removed the bags a further 35 miles to Leesville, where he stored them in an empty house. "Worn out with his labors, Mr. Pleasonton states in a letter, he retired early to bed that night and slept soundly. Next morning he was informed by the people of the little tavern where he had stayed that evening that they had seen during the night, the same being the 24th of August, a large fire in the direction of Washington, which proved to be the light from the public buildings, which the enemy had set on fire and burned to the ground."

• • •

THREEFER

MINE (English), MIEN (French), and MEIN (German) are synonyms and anagrams in three languages.

• • •

ALPHABET BLOCKS

We have 27 wooden cubes. The first is marked A on every face, the second B, and so on through the alphabet to Z. The 27th cube is blank. Is it possible to assemble these cubes into a 3×3×3 cube with the blank cube at the center, arranging them so that cube A adjoins cube B, cube B adjoins cube C, and so on, forming a connected orthogonal path through the alphabet?

(See Answers and Solutions)

• • •

SUGAR AND SPICE

Excerpts from the essays of 19th-century schoolboys, from Caroline Bigelow Le Row's *English as She Is Taught*, 1887:

"Girls are very stuckup and dignefied in their maner and behaveyour. They think more of dress than anything and like to play with dowls and rags. They cry if they see a cow in afar distance and are afraid of guns. They stay at home all the time and go to Church every Sunday. They are al-ways sick. They are always funy and making fun of boys hands and they say how dirty. They cant play marbels. I pity them poor things. They make fun of boys and then turn round and love them. I dont beleave they ever kiled a cat or any thing. They look out every nite and say oh ant the moon lovely. Thir is one thing I have not told and that is they always now their lessons bettern boys."

"Timidity is a disease very prevelent among our American women. It is thought by them to be an ornament to their charms. How many young women faint by the sudden appearance of a rat from its hideing place! Oh! they do declare it's impossible to live where these dreadful creatures make their homes they ask Ma cant she and wont she please to try to secure some remedy so they can be destroyed. You will see the young ladies leap up over stones and steps of great height so as to escape the barks of the dog, if they are walking with a friend of the male kind they will cling to the masculine arm and beseach him to walk so that she might loose sight of that horrible creature known as a dog."

• • •

PRINCE AND MISPRINTS

In 1889 Fredericka Beardsley Gilchrist advanced a theory that the entire meaning of *Hamlet* has been confused because of a typographical error. In Act I, Scene V, the ghost reveals to Hamlet his mother's adultery and his father's murder. Hamlet responds:

O all you host of heaven! O earth! what else?
And shall I couple hell? O fie!

Gilchrist maintains that the second line should read:

And shall I couple? Hell! O fie!

In other words, "And after this shall I also marry? No!" He gives up his love for Ophelia, and the rest of the play is the story of "an unhappy lover."

For Gilchrist this is "the one key that unlocks every difficulty in the play": "For nearly three hundred years it has been possible to misunderstand, not special passages only, but the fundamental intention of the play; during that time no satisfactory explanation of all its obscurities has been advanced. I believe this theory explains them; and this belief, based on careful study and comparison, ought to excuse the seeming vanity and presumption of the preceding statement."

• • •

"MUSIC AND BALDNESS"

❝❝An English statistician has recently been engaged in an original task, that of studying the influence of music on the hair. . . . While stringed instruments prevent and check the falling out of the hair, brass instruments have the most injurious effects upon it. The piano and the violin, especially the piano, have an undoubted preserving influence. The violoncello, the harp, and the double bass participate in the hair-preserving qualities of the piano. But the hautboy, the clarinet, and the Mute have only a very feeble effect. Their action is not more than a fiftieth part as strong. On the contrary, the brass instruments have results that are deplorable.

—*Scientific American*, Aug. 29, 1896

(Summarizing the same study, the *Boston Medical and Surgical Journal* reported that "brass instruments have a fatal influence on the growth of the hair, notably the cornet, the French horn, and the trombone, which apparently will depilate a player's scalp in less than five years. . . . The baldness which prevails among members of regimental bands has been given the name of 'trumpet baldness,' *calvitié des fanfares*.")

• • •

UNQUOTE

"The animal needing something knows how
much it needs, the man does not."

—Democritus

• • •

EN GARDE!

The modern pentathlon comprises five events: show jumping, fencing, 200-meter freestyle swimming, pistol shooting, and a 3-kilometer cross-country run.

Pierre de Coubertin, the founder of the modern Olympic Games, conceived the sport to reflect the skills needed by a Napoleonic cavalry officer: He must ride across unfamiliar terrain; engage an opponent at swordpoint; swim a river that his steed cannot cross; exchange fire with his enemies; and run across country.

Coubertin believed that this event, more than any other, "tested an athlete's moral qualities as much as their physical resources and skills, producing thereby the ideal, complete athlete."

• • •

A MORE PERFECT UNION

The names of the 48 contiguous United States fall neatly into
the two halves of the alphabet:

Alabama	Nebraska
Arizona	Nevada
Arkansas	New Hampshire
California	New Jersey
Colorado	New Mexico
Connecticut	New York
Delaware	North Carolina
Florida	North Dakota
Georgia	Ohio
Idaho	Oklahoma
Illinois	Oregon
Indiana	Pennsylvania
Iowa	Rhode Island
Kansas	South Carolina
Kentucky	South Dakota
Louisiana	Tennessee
Maine	Texas
Maryland	Utah
Massachusetts	Vermont
Michigan	Virginia
Minnesota	Washington
Mississippi	West Virginia
Missouri	Wisconsin
Montana	Wyoming

16 start with A-L, 16 with M-N, and 16 with O-Z.

• • •

NON-FICTION

Sherlock Holmes is an honorary fellow of the Royal Society of Chemistry.

"Holmes did not exist, but he should have existed," society chief David Giachardi said in bestowing the award in 2002. "That is how important he is to our culture. We contend that the Sherlock Holmes myth is now so deeply rooted in the national and international psyche through books, films, radio and television that he has almost transcended fictional boundaries."

• • •

VINDICATED

As a writer, W.T. Stead may have been too prescient.

In 1886 he published an article about the sinking of an ocean liner and the consequent loss of life, warning, "This is exactly what might take place and will take place if liners are sent to sea short of boats."

Six years later he wrote a novel, *From the Old World to the New*, in which a ship collides with an iceberg in the North Atlantic and sinks; the survivors are picked up by the *Majestic*, a ship of the White Star Line.

An outspoken newspaper editor, Stead himself embarked for the New World in April 1912 when President Taft invited him to address a peace conference at Carnegie Hall.

Alas, he never arrived—he had booked his passage on the RMS *Titanic*.

• • •

"STEALING THE BELL ROPES"

A puzzle by Henry Dudeney:

      “A robber broke into the belfry of a church, and though he had nothing to assist him but his pocket-knife, he contrived to steal nearly the complete lengths of the two bell-ropes, which passed through holes in the lofty boarded ceiling. How did he effect his purpose? Of course, there was no ladder or aught else to assist him. It is easy to understand that he might steal one rope and slide down the other, but how he cut the two, or any considerable portion of them, without a bad fall, is perplexing.

(See Answers and Solutions)

• • •

WEIGHT WATCHERS

The Habeas Corpus Act of 1679 is a landmark in English law, permitting a prisoner to challenge the lawfulness of his detention. But Parliament passed it through an absurd miscount:

      “Lord Grey and Lord Norris were named to be the tellers: Lord Norris, being a man subject to vapours, was not at all times attentive to what he was doing: so, a very fat lord coming in, Lord Grey counted him as ten, as a jest at first: but seeing Lord Norris had not observed it, he went on with this misreckoning of ten: so it was reported that they that were for the Bill were in the majority, though indeed it went for the other side: and by this means the Bill passed.

That account, by contemporary historian Gilbert Burnet, is borne out by the session minutes. The act remains on the statute book to this day.

• • •

BEYOND THE PALE

Expressions banned from use in New Zealand parliamentary debate:

1933
Blowfly-minded

1943
Retardate worm

1946
Clown of the House
Idle vapourings of a mind diseased
I would cut the honourable gentleman's throat if I had the
    chance

1949
His brains could revolve inside a peanut shell for a thousand
    years without touching the sides

1957
Kind of animal that gnaws holes

1959
Member not fit to lick the shoes of the Prime Minister

1963
Energy of a tired snail returning home from a funeral

1966
Shut up yourself, you great ape
Snotty-nosed little boy
You are a cheap little twerp
Ridiculous mouse

1974
Could go down the Mount Eden sewer and come up cleaner
than he went in
Dreamed the bill up in the bath
Frustrated warlord

In brighter news, saying that a fellow member "scuttles for
his political funk hole" was deemed allowable in 1974.

• • •

"A POEM"

Be good, be good, be always good,
And now & then be clever,
But don't you ever be too good,
Nor ever be too clever;
For such as be too awful good
They awful lonely are,
And such as often clever be
Get cut & stung & trodden on by persons of lesser mental
capacity, for this kind do by a law of their construction regard
exhibitions of superior intellectuality as an offensive imperti-

nence leveled at their lack of this high gift, & are prompt to resent such-like exhibitions in the manner above indicated—& are they justifiable? alas, alas they

(It is not best to go on; I think the line is already longer than it ought to be for real true poetry.)

—Mark Twain

• • •

UNDISTURBED

Periander ordered two young men to go out by night along a certain road, to kill the first man they met there, and to bury him.

Then he ordered four more men to find those two and kill them. And he sent an even greater number to murder those four.

Periander then set off down the road himself to wait for them.

In this way he ensured that the location of his grave would never be known.

• • •

SMALL TALK

❝A gentleman sitting in one of the boxes in company with the late Lord North, not knowing his lordship, entered into conversation with him, and, seeing two ladies come into an opposite box, turned to him, and addressed him with, 'Pray, sir, can you inform me who is that ugly woman that is just come in?' 'O,' replied his lordship, with great good humor, 'that is my wife.' 'Sir, I ask you ten thousand pardons;

I do not mean her, I mean that shocking monster who is along with her.' 'That,' replied his lordship, 'is my daughter.'

—M. Lafayette Byrn, *The Repository of Wit and Humor*, 1853

• • •

THE ANSWER WHEEL

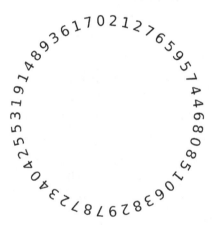

Multiply 212765957446808510638297872340425531914893617 by any number from 2 to 46 and you'll find the product on the ring above.

Einstein wrote, "Pure mathematics is, in its way, the poetry of logical ideas."

• • •

THE GHOST PLANE

On Dec. 8, 1942, American forces in Kienow, China, spotted an unidentified plane heading toward them on a beeline from Formosa. Pilots Bob Scott and Johnny Hampshire approached it and discovered it was an old American P-40B Tomahawk bearing an insignia that hadn't been seen since Pearl Harbor. The pilot would not identify himself.

Fearing a trick by the Japanese, Scott and Hampshire fired briefly on the plane, but it sought neither to evade them nor to counterattack. Scott moved to the plane's farther side and saw that it had been badly damaged before they came upon it—the canopy had been shot away, the right aileron was gone, and part of the wing was missing. The pilot's head was slumped on his chest. Strangest of all, the P-40B had no landing gear—the wheel wells were empty.

Scott and Hampshire lost the plane in a cloud bank and then saw it crash in a rice paddy below. Who was the pilot, and where had the strange plane come from? No one knows, but after years of research Scott evolved a conjecture that it had been assembled by a small group of Air Corps personnel who had retreated from Bataan to Corregidor and then to Mindanao. If this is true it must have flown more than 1,000 miles through enemy airspace to reach China.

Japanese records confirm that there was an American P-40 over Formosa on Dec. 8, 1942, but where it came from, where it was headed, and indeed how it even got airborne remain a mystery.

• • •

LOGIC

❝John-a-Nokes was driving his Cart toward Croydon, and by the Way fell asleep therein: Mean time a Thief came by and stole his two Horses, and went quite away with them; In the End he awaking, and missing them, said, Either I am

John a Nokes, or I am not John a Nokes. If I am John a Nokes, then have I lost two Horses; and if I be not John a Nokes, then have I found a Cart.

—*The Jester's Magazine,* February 1766

• • •

IN A WORD

kakopygian
adj. having ugly buttocks

ostreophagist
n. an eater of oysters

preantepenultimate
adj. fourth from last

charrette
n. a final, intensive effort to finish a project before a deadline

• • •

WARM WORDS

❝It is said that, when Charles Dudley Warner was the editor of the 'Hartford Press,' back in the 'sixties,' arousing the patriotism of the State with his vigorous appeals, one of the type-setters came in from the composing-room, and, planting himself before the editor, said: 'Well, Mr. Warner, I've decided to enlist in the army.' With mingled sensations of pride and responsibility, Mr. Warner replied encouragingly that he was glad to see the man felt the call of duty. 'Oh, it isn't that,' said the truthful compositor, 'but I'd rather be shot than try to set any more of your damned copy.'

—John Wilson, "The Importance of the Proof-Reader," 1901

• • •

THE ABSENCE PARADOX

If you are somewhere else, you are not here.
You are not in Rome; you are somewhere else.
Therefore you are not here.

• • •

SYMMETRY

Reversing the Dutch word for kidney, NIER, gives the French word for kidney, REIN.

• • •

TAKEOUT FOOD

Here's a theological poser: What happens to cannibals on Judgment Day? If I eat you and assimilate your flesh, how can we both be resurrected?

"It is not possible for two men to be resurrected with the same flesh at the same time, and nor is it possible for the same limb to have two different masters," writes Athenagoras of Athens. "How can two bodies, which have successively been in possession of the same substance, appear in their entirety, without lacking a large part of themselves? In the end, either the disputed parts will be returned to their original owners, leaving a gap in the later owners, or they shall be fixed in the latter, leaving in this case an irreparable loss in the former." Augustine answers, "The flesh in question shall be restored to the man in whom it first became human flesh; for it is to be considered as borrowed of the other man, and, like borrowed money, to be returned to him from whom it was taken."

I guess we'll find out.

• • •

LATE BLOOMER

Gioachino Rossini was born on a leap day, Feb. 29, 1792. Because 1800 was not a leap year, he took 12 years to reach his second birthday.

• • •

INSULT TO INJURY

Anthony Burgess wrote his Enderby novels under the pen name Joseph Kell. So he was amused when in 1963 the *Yorkshire Post* asked him to review one of them.

Sensing a practical joke by one of the editors, he submitted a scathing review. "This is in many ways a dirty book," he wrote. "It may well make some people sick, and those of my readers with tender stomachs are advised to let it alone."

Alas, the assignment wasn't a joke. The newspaper published Burgess' review—and when it discovered his double identity, "I was attacked by the editor of the *Yorkshire Post* on Yorkshire Television and promptly, and perhaps justly, dismissed."

• • •

WHEREVER

At the height of Mark Twain's popularity, a group of his friends in New York wanted to send him a birthday greeting.

But Twain was traveling abroad and none of them knew where to direct the letter.

After some hopeless havering they simply addressed it "Mark Twain, God Knows Where."

Several weeks later a note arrived from Twain.

It said: "He did."

• • •

STOPPING BY

In the film *Lifeboat*, the action is set entirely in a small boat. This left director Alfred Hitchcock momentarily at a loss how to make his traditional cameo appearance.

Finally, inspired by a recent diet, he hit on a solution—Hitchcock can be seen briefly in a newspaper advertisement for "Reduco, the Obesity Slayer."

• • •

KILLING WITH KINDNESS

❝A faded and somewhat droll survival of ecclesiastical excommunication and exorcism is the custom, still prevailing in European countries and some portions of the United States, of serving a writ of ejectment on rats or simply sending them a friendly letter of advice in order to induce them to quit any house, in which their presence is deemed undesirable. Lest the rats should overlook and thus fail to read the epistle, it is rubbed with grease, so as to attract their attention, rolled up and thrust into their holes. Mr. William Wells Newell, in a paper on 'Conjuring Rats,' printed in The Journal of American Folk-Lore (Jan.-March, 1892), gives a specimen of such a letter, dated, 'Maine, Oct. 31, 1888,' and addressed in business style to 'Messrs. Rats and Co.' The writer begins by expressing his deep interest in the welfare of said rats as well as his fears lest they should find their winter quarters in No. 1, Seaview Street, uncomfortable and poorly supplied with suitable food, since it is only a summer residence and is also about to undergo repairs. He then suggests that they migrate to No. 6, Incubator Street, where they 'can live snug and happy' in a splendid cellar well stored with vegetables of all kinds and can pass easily through a shed leading to a barn containing much grain. He concludes by stating that he will do them no harm if they heed his advice, otherwise he shall be forced to use 'Rough on Rats.' This threat of resorting to rat poison in case of the refusal to accept his kind counsel is all that remains of the once formidable anathema of the Church.

—E.P. Evans, *The Criminal Prosecution and Capital Punishment of Animals*, 1906

• • •

PURPLE MOUNTAINS

Excerpts from an Independence Day oration by Nashville attorney Edwin H. Tenney to the Young Men's Association of Great Bend, Tenn., July 4, 1858:

- "Venerable, my Fellow Citizens, on the brilliant calendar of American Independence, is the day we celebrate. Venerable as the revolving epoch in our anniversaries of freedom is this avalanche of time. Venerable as the abacus on the citadel of greatness, thou well-spring of hope. Homestead of Liberty, we venerate thy habitation. Monument of immortality, we adorate thy worth."

- "To those veterans eulogy is preposterous and monuments unavailing, but a heart soaking with gratitude is never bleak nor serene. Cold calumny may chill it and life's icicles freeze it, but when thawed by recollections blood leaps through its veins. Could we learn from immortality their fame or presage their memory, the priceless league—the serried rank—the siren yell—the solemn march—the cracking bone—the flying flesh—the clinic pang—the grilling wail—the quenchless sigh and the clattering footsteps of that army welding sympathy to ages and liberty to life, will float like the dying groans of Calvary down the rapids of mortality, and whistling salvation along the whirlpool of nations, they will enter like their fathers a sea of bliss."

- "Such a theme needs no epitasis. It needs no amphitheatre with its Ignatius irritating the lions to accelerate his glory. It needs not the inflexibility of a Laurentius—or the suavity of a Pionius for its apodosis."

- "Some of our ladies find this romance 'mid flounces and ostentation—'mid luxury and expense—'mid smatterers of French peppered with Latin; of Latin salted with Greek; or of Greek hashed with German. To petrify their brains with problems or dishes would be blowing up the ramparts of beauty and fortune; pillaging the flower pots of geranium magnificence, and insulting the bounties of a benevolent God."

- "Would you remove these Senacheribs from Amaranthus—then become Malanchthons in reforms not Catalines of your country. Better banish—like Lycurgus—politician and poet rather than not tear from our wheels this drag-chain of Romance which is the pabulum of fancy and nursery of woe."

"What does he mean by 'blowing up the ramparts of beauty?'" wondered the *Daily Alta California* afterward. "The obscurity can't be in the writer, and must therefore lie in our own ignorance. Still we ask—what are the ramparts of beauty?"

• • •

A VERSATILE PALINDROME

From Royal V. Heath in *Scripta Mathematica*, March 1955:

$$0264 + 4125 + 5610 = 0165 + 5214 + 4620$$

. . . remains valid if you split each term with a multiplication sign:

$$02 \times 64 + 41 \times 25 + 56 \times 10 = 01 \times 65 + 52 \times 14 + 46 \times 20$$

. . . or an addition sign:

$$02 + 64 + 41 + 25 + 56 + 10 = 01 + 65 + 52 + 14 + 46 + 20$$

Remarkably, everything above holds true if you square each term.

• • •

THE JACKASS OF VANVRES

In 1750, Jacques Ferron was caught having sex with an ass and sentenced to death.

To add insult to injury, the ass had a character witness:

66 The prior to the convent. . . and the principal inhabitants of the commune of Vanvres signed a certificate stating that they had known the said she-ass for four years, and that she had always shown herself to be virtuous and well-behaved both at home and abroad and had never given occasion of scandal to any one, and that therefore 'they were willing to bear witness that she is in word and deed and in all her habits of life a most honest creature.'

The ass was acquitted and Ferron hanged.

• • •

FUN WITH LOGS

Google's 2004 IPO announced it intended to raise $2,718,281,828. That's *e* to 9 decimal places.

• • •

SHIBBOLETH

Isaac Asimov proposed a simple way to distinguish chemists from non-chemists: Ask them to read aloud the word *unionized*.

Non-chemists will pronounce it "union-ized", he said—and chemists will pronounce it "un-ionized."

• • •

DAMN REBS

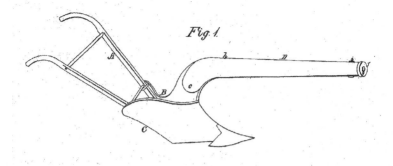

Fig 1.

A combination plow and cannon, patented in 1862 by C.M. French and W.H. Fancher:

❝❝As a piece of light ordnance its capacity may vary from a projectile of one to three pounds weight without rendering it cumbersome as a plow. Its utility as an implement of the twofold capacity described is unquestionable, especially when used in border localities, subject to savage feuds and guerrilla warfare.

"As a means of defense in repelling surprises and skirmishing attacks on those engaged in a peaceful avocation it is unrivaled."

• • •

MAKING WAY

A man is 4/7 across a train trestle when he sees a train coming. To get off the trestle, he can run toward the train or away from it. As it happens, in either case he'll reach safety just as the locomotive passes him. If he runs at 20 kph, how fast is the train going?

(See Answers and Solutions)

• • •

A LOOK AHEAD

On the occasion of the 1893 World's Fair, the American Press Association asked 74 prominent Americans to imagine the United States of 1993. Some responses:

- "By the 1990s, longevity will be so improved that 150 years will be no unusual age to reach."—Thomas De Witt Talmage, Presbyterian preacher
- "In the 1990s, the United States will be a government of perhaps 60 states, situated in both North and South America."—Asa C. Matthews, comptroller of the Treasury
- "Wealth will be more widely and equally distributed. Great corporations and business interests will be conducted harmoniously—on the principle of the employers and workers sharing in the profits."—Junius Henri Browne, journalist
- "Three hours will constitute a long day's work."—Mary E. Lease, activist and lecturer
- "Trousers will be relegated to bookkeepers, barbers, pastry bakers, and cripples."—Van Buren Denslow, attorney and economist
- "We are going to see a wonderful development in the use of jewels in American churches."—George F. Kunz, mineralogist
- "By the end of the Twentieth Century, taxation will be reduced to a minimum, the entire world will be open to trade, and there will be no need of a standing army."—Erastus Wiman, journalist

"Perhaps I am wrong in some of these prophecies," reflected drama critic John Habberton, who had predicted that all marriages would be happy. "But if that is so, I shall not be here to be twitted with it—now will I?"

PART SEVEN

CHIMNEYS, ASPARAGUS,
and **ROBINSON CRUSOE**

ON TIME

In Max Beerbohm's 1916 short story "Enoch Soames," an unsuccessful poet sells his soul to the devil for the chance to travel 100 years into the future to see how time has favored his work. Under the agreement, Soames is transported to the Reading Room of the British Museum at 2:10 p.m. on June 3, 1997. He searches for references to his work but finds himself mentioned only once, as an "imaginary character" in a story by Max Beerbohm, and is whisked off to hell.

But, Beerbohm writes, "You realize that the reading-room into which Soames was projected by the devil was in all respects precisely as it will be on the afternoon of June 3, 1997. You realize, therefore, that on that afternoon, when it comes round, there the selfsame crowd will be, and there Soames will be, punctually. . . . The fact that people are going to stare at him and follow him around and seem afraid of him, can be explained only on the hypothesis that they will somehow have been prepared for his ghostly visitation."

On June 3, 1997, about a dozen onlookers collected in the Reading Room of the British Museum to see what would happen. To their surprise, at precisely 2:10 p.m. a man matching Soames' description—"a stooping, shambling person, rather tall, very pale, with longish and brownish hair"—appeared and began to search catalogs and speak with the librarians. Dejected, he finally disappeared among the stacks.

Among the onlookers was Teller, of the magician duo Penn & Teller.

• • •

SECOND CHANCES

66A man was hanged who had cut his throat, but who had been brought back to life. They hanged him for suicide. The doctor had warned them that it was impossible to hang him as the throat would burst open and he would breathe through the aperture. They did not listen to his advice and hanged their man. The wound in the neck immediately opened and the man came back to life again although he was hanged. It took time to convoke the aldermen to decide the question of what was to be done. At length the aldermen assembled and bound up the neck below the wound until he died. O my Mary, what a crazy society and what a stupid civilization.

—Russian exile Nicholas Ogarev, writing to his English mistress Mary Sutherland, 1860

• • •

NUMERIUS NEGIDIUS

Only 43 numbers have names that lack the letter N. One of them, fittingly, is forty-three.

• • •

AN INVITATION

On Nov. 25, 1862, Abraham Lincoln sent this dispatch to Gen. Ambrose Burnside at Aquia Creek, Va.:

Can Inn Ale me withe 2 oar our Ann pas Ann me flesh ends NV

Corn Inn out with U cud Inn heaven day nest Wed roe Moore Tom darkey hat Greek Why Hawk of abbott Inn B chewed I if.
What did it mean?

(See Answers and Solutions)

• • •

WHAT?

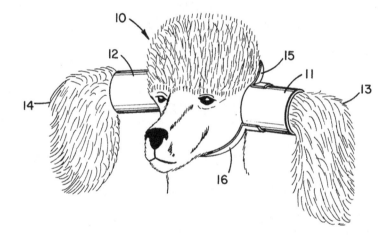

James D. Williams' "animal ear protectors," patented in 1980, provide "a device for protecting the ears of animals, especially long-haired dogs, from becoming soiled by the animal's food while the animal is eating." The ears are protected by plastic tubes that are held to the animal's head by adjustable straps.

The invention "may be itself decorated so as to enhance the appearance of the animal in the eyes of its owner and of others." What that looks like is left to the imagination.

• • •

THE SHOE FITS

William F. Buckley Jr. called Norman Mailer an egotist, "almost unique in his search for notoriety and absolutely unequalled in his co-existence with it."

Mailer called Buckley a "second-rate intellect incapable of entertaining two serious thoughts in a row."

In 1966 Buckley sent Mailer an autographed copy of *The Unmaking of a Mayor*, the memoir of his unsuccessful run for mayor of New York City the previous year.

Mailer turned to the index and looked up his own name. There he found, in Buckley's handwriting, the words "Hi, Norman."

• • •

HOUSE CALL

Letter from Charles Dickens to a chimney sweep, March 15, 1864:

 Dear Sir,

Since you last swept my study chimney it has developed some peculiar eccentricities. Smoke has indeed proceeded from the cowl that surmounts it, but it has seemingly been undergoing internal agonies of a most distressing nature, and pours forth disastrous volumes of swarthy vapour into the apartment wherein I habitually labour. Although a comforting relief probably to the chimney, this is not altogether convenient to me. If you can send a confidential sub-sweep, with whom the chimney can engage in social intercourse, it might be induced to disclose the cause of the departure from its normal functions.

Faithfully yours,
Charles Dickens

• • •

DEAD LETTERS

In a trance in 1926, medium Geraldine Cummins wrote out messages transmitted to her by a disembodied spirit who had died 1900 years earlier. Architect Frederick Bligh Bond transcribed, punctuated, and arranged the messages. When Bond published these in a newspaper, Cummins sued him. This raises an interesting legal question: Who holds the copyright?

In an extempore judgment, Justice J. Eve wrote that, although all parties agreed that "the true originator of all that is found in these documents is some being no longer inhabiting this world," the medium's "active cooperation" had helped to translate them into modern language. This might make her a joint author with the disembodied spirit, but "recognizing as I do that I have no jurisdiction extending to the sphere in which he moves," he found that "authorship rests with this lady."

Bond had claimed that the writing had no living author, that, in Eve's words, "the authorship and copyright rest with some one already domiciled on the other side of the inevitable river." But "That is a matter I must leave for solution by others more competent to decide it than I am. I can only look upon the matter as a terrestrial one, of the earth earthy, and I propose to deal with it on that footing. In my opinion the plaintiff has made out her case, and the copyright rests with her."

• • •

EXTENDED TOUR

In 1938, 18-year-old Korean soldier Yang Kyoungjong was conscripted into the Japanese army to fight against the Soviet Union.

He was captured by the Red Army, which pressed him into fighting the Nazis on the eastern front.

In 1943 he was captured by the Germans, who forced him to fight the invading Allies at Normandy.

There he was captured by American paratroopers in June 1944.

This means he fought for three different armies during World War II, and was captured each time. He died in Illinois in 1992.

• • •

GENE POOL

Asked whether he would give his life to save a drowning brother, J.B.S. Haldane said, "No, but I would to save two brothers or eight cousins."

• • •

RULES OF THUMB

"If an elderly but distinguished scientist says that something is possible he is almost certainly right, but if he says that it is impossible he is very probably wrong."—Arthur C. Clarke

"When, however, the lay public rallies around an idea that is denounced by distinguished but elderly scientists and supports that idea with great fervor and emotion—the distinguished but elderly scientists are then, after all, probably right."—Isaac Asimov

• • •

BEST-LAID PLANS

Launched in November 1981, the Soviet Union's Venera 14 probe carried a spring-loaded arm to test the soil of Venus. The craft journeyed for four lonely months to reach its destination, descended safely through the hostile atmosphere, and landed securely on the surface. The spring-loaded arm plunged downward—into a camera lens cap, which had just fallen there.

• • •

AN EPIGRAMMATIC PUZZLE

Nokes went, he thought, to Styles's wife to bed,
Nor knew his own was laid there in her stead;
Civilian, is the child then begot
To be allow'd legitimate or not?

—*Bon Ton Magazine*, July 1794

• • •

IN A WORD

circumforaneous
adj. wandering from house to house

dentiloquy
n. speech through gritted teeth

imparlibidinous
adj. pertaining to an unequal state of desire between two
  people

quinquiplicate
v. to multiply by five

• • •

CAT AND MOUSE

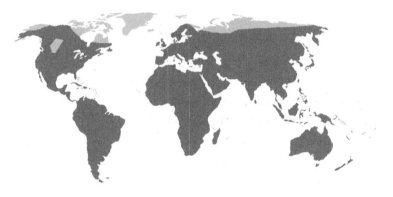

Rats have pretty well overrun the globe, but there's one excep-
tion: Alberta, Canada, which has waged a successful war against
the critters for 50 years. Owning rats is forbidden to Alberta residents; they can be kept only by zoos and research institutions.
The province maintains a rat control zone 600 kilometers long
along its eastern border, staffed by eight professionals, and any
rats they find are poisoned, gassed, or shot.

"Alberta is the only province with rat-free status, and we take
this very seriously," said Verlyn Olson, minister of agriculture
and rural development. "We have lived without the menace of
rats since 1950, when our control program began."

But it's a constant battle. In 2003 pest specialist John B.

Bourne told *National Geographic* that he worries the wily creatures will hitch a ride to the interior aboard a truck or train. "They are so adaptive, so intelligent, so successful and physically capable . . . that it would not surprise me if they show up in a place where you'd least expect a rat to show up. I have the greatest respect for this rodent's resourcefulness, and [its] capabilities scare the hell out of me."

• • •

QUICK!

Obey this command!

• • •

A NIGHT VISIT

In the little town of Villisca, Iowa, 35-year-old Joe Moore, his wife, his four children, and two visiting daughters of a neighbor went to bed on June 9, 1912.

The following morning, all eight were dead.

"The parties were all killed with an axe which was found in the house, the axe belonging to Mr. Moore," reported Iowa attorney general Horace Havner. "The window shades were all drawn and the doors covered with clothing so that no light could get out from the house. The mirrors in the house were also all covered. Not one of the parties received any injury below the neck but the heads of the victims were all beaten to a pulp, the head of Mr. Moore being mangled worse than the rest, although they were all beaten beyond the possibility of recognition."

Ten years of investigations, grand juries, trials, and arguments produced no convictions. The case remains unsolved.

• • •

FAITH AND REASON

Jean Buridan presented a logical proof of the existence of God:

God exists.
Neither of these sentences is true.

The two statements can be reconciled only if God exists.

• • •

SPUD LOOPS

Given any pair of potatoes—even bizarre, Richard Nixon-shaped potatoes—it's always possible to draw a loop on each so that the two loops are identical in three dimensions.

Do you see the simple, intuitive proof for this?

(See Answers and Solutions)

• • •

FIRST TO MARKET

In March 1964, David Threlfall sent a unique request to book-maker William Hill: "I'd like to bet £10 that a man will set foot on the surface of the moon before the first of January 1970."

He'd heard President Kennedy's 1961 address challenging the United States to put a man on the moon by the end of the decade, and "I thought if a bookmaker was prepared to offer reasonable odds it would be a commonsense bet."

The bookmaker disagreed and put the odds at 1,000 to 1. Threlfall accepted, and the bet was placed on April 10.

As the Apollo program advanced, the odds began to drop, and people began to offer Threlfall thousands of pounds for his betting slip. He held on to it, though, and when Neil Armstrong set foot on the moon in 1969, he received the reward for his fore-thought—a check for £10,000.

• • •

TOO TRUE

Secretary: It must be hard to lose your mother-in-law.
W.C. Fields: Yes, it is, very hard. It's almost impossible.

• • •

IMAGINARY LOVER

In a letter, Lewis Carroll asked his sister to analyze a little girl's reasoning:
"I'm so glad I don't like asparagus—because, if I did like it, I should have to eat it—and I can't bear it!"
Carroll added: "It bothers me considerably."

• • •

OOPS

In 1950, Stanford graduate student Robert E. Young realized that two chapters of Henry James' novel *The Ambassadors* had been reversed in every American edition since 1903.

"Various discrepancies in facts and time are apparent on careful reading of the chapters in their present order," he wrote. "On the other hand, the reversal of the two results in the complete elimination of these discrepancies."

It turned out that the two chapters appeared in the opposite order in the English editions, and many American publishers adopted that order accordingly.

But James himself had not noted any error in revising the American text in 1909, and it's possible to view that version as correct and the English text as reversed, if one allows for some chronological inconsistency.

The result is that there is no definitive text. "The mishap is particularly ironic," Young wrote, "in view of the fact that James regarded *The Ambassadors* as his most perfectly constructed novel, his masterpiece."

• • •

PHONE SECTS

WELL-EXPRESSED is dialed using only the odd numbers on a telephone keypad.

NONCOMMUNICATING uses only even numbers.

Surely this means something.

• • •

A GUILTY FACE

One morning in 1727, York pubkeeper Hannah Williams found that her writing desk had been opened and a sum of money stolen. As waiter Thomas Geddely disappeared at the same time, there was little doubt as to the robber.

Twelve months later, a man calling himself James Crow arrived in York and took a job as a porter. The townspeople immediately accosted him as Geddely, but he insisted that he didn't know them, that his name was James Crow, and that he was new to York.

Williams was called for, instantly identified him as Geddely, and accused him of robbing her. The man protested his innocence before a justice of the peace but had no alibi and admitted to a history as a vagabond and a petty rogue. At the trial a servant testified that she had seen him at the robbery scene with a poker in his hand. He swore again that his name was James Crow but was convicted and executed.

Some time later Thomas Geddely was arrested in Dublin on a robbery charge. While in custody he confessed to the robbery at York. A York resident who was visiting Ireland at the time declared that the resemblance between the two men was so great "that it was next to impossible for the nicest eye to have distinguished their persons asunder."

• • •

ALL DRESSED UP

The shortest named speaking role in Shakespeare is that of Taurus in *Antony and Cleopatra*.

He says, "My lord?"

• • •

UNQUOTE

"If the triangles made a god, they would give him three sides."—Montesquieu

• • •

SCALE DEGREES

❝Suppose that in one night all the dimensions of the universe became a thousand times larger. The world will remain *similar* to itself, if we give the word *similitude* the meaning it has in the third book of Euclid. Only, what was formerly a meter long will now measure a kilometer, and what was a millimeter long will become a meter. The bed in which I went to sleep and my body itself will have grown in the same proportion. When I wake in the morning what will be my feeling in face of such an astonishing transformation? Well, I shall not notice anything at all. The most exact measures will be incapable of revealing anything of this tremendous change, since the yard-measures I shall use will have varied in exactly the same proportions as the objects I shall attempt to measure.

—Henri Poincaré, *Science and Method*, 1908

• • •

TYPE TALK

In April 1977, as a joke, the British newspaper *The Guardian* published a seven-page supplement about a fictional island nation called San Serriffe. It fooled quite a few readers, which is surprising, since it's essentially a series of bad puns about typography:

- There are two main islands, the Upper Caisse and the Lower Caisse. The capital, Bodoni, is linked by highways to the major ports, including Port Clarendon, but Arial in the Lower Caisse has grown in importance during the personal computer era.
- Natives are called Flong, and the descendants of colonists are known as colons. Those of mixed race are called semicolons.
- At independence in 1967, the country was led by General Pica, a military strongman.
- Cultural highlights include the Ampersand String Quartet and "Times Nude Romances."

- The islands hold an annual endurance challenge race, known as the Two Em Dash, that now attracts international participants.

The island's alternate name, if it needed any, is Hoaxe.

• • •

LIMERICK

There was a young lady named Psyche
Who was heard to ejaculate, "Pcryche!"
For, riding her pbych,
She ran over a ptych,
And fell on some rails that were pspyche.

• • •

RUMORS OF MY DEATH. . .

Physicist James Van Allen outlived his own obituary writer.

As Van Allen approached old age, the Associated Press assigned writer Walter Sullivan to prepare a story that could be published on his death. Sullivan did so and died in 1996, but his story sat in the file for 10 more years before Van Allen finally passed away at 91.

• • •

THE BARBER'S DICTUM

Let's say that the densest human head of hair contains 200,000 strands, and that the human population is 6 billion. That means there's a group of at least 30,000 people today who have precisely the same number of hairs on their heads.

Do you see why?

• • •

AN INVISIBLE MAP

Shot down over South Vietnam in 1972, Air Force navigator Iceal Hambleton needed to reach the Cam Lo River but was surrounded by enemy forces who might intercept any radio messages sent to him. After some consultation, rescuers told him to play the first hole at the Tucson National Golf Course. "Before you start be damned sure you line your shot up properly," they said. "Very bad traps on this hole."

Hambleton was bewildered at first but came to understand. As an avid golfer he was familiar with a number of American courses, and he had a photographic memory of each hole's length and layout. The first hole at Tucson was 430 yards long and ran southeast, so he set off accordingly across country, following an imaginary fairway.

This worked. By invoking additional holes from three Air Force bases, as well as a par 3 from Augusta National, rescuers led Hambleton to the river, where a Navy SEAL picked him up.

"Two things kept me alive," he told *Golf Digest* in 2001. "The will to live, and my wife. And we're playing golf Friday."

• • •

PRIVATE LINE

In 1980, Morris Davie was accused of setting forest fires and brought to the headquarters of the Royal Canadian Mounted Police to take a lie detector test. He was left alone in a room, where a hidden camera recorded him dropping to his knees and saying, "Oh God, let me get away with it just this once."

At trial, his lawyer objected to this evidence, arguing that it violated a Canadian law that prohibited the interception of private communications "made under circumstances in which it is reasonable for the originator thereof to expect that it will not be intercepted by any person other than the person intended by the originator thereof to receive it."

Is God a person? The trial judge thought so—he held the videotape inadmissible and Davie was acquitted. The British Columbia Court of Appeal disagreed, however, deciding that a private communication requires an "intended human recipient."

"In my opinion," wrote Justice J.A. Hutcheon, "the word 'person' is used in the statutes of Canada to describe someone to whom rights are granted and upon whom obligations are placed. There is no earthly authority which can grant rights or impose duties upon God. I can find no reason to think that the Parliament of Canada has attempted to do so in the enactment of sections of the Criminal Code dealing with the protection of privacy." He ordered a new trial.

• • •

ANONYMOUS

Who wrote *The Treasure of the Sierra Madre*? Strangely, no one knows. The novel is credited to B. Traven, but exactly who that is has been a matter of speculation for more than 80 years.

Most of Traven's output was published between 1926 and 1939, composed in German sprinkled with Americanisms and frequently concerning leftist politics and Mexican history.

The writer himself never came forward, and he left only intriguing clues to his identity: In the 1920s apparently he was associated with Munich anarchist Erich Mühsam, and later a Mexican journalist discovered a bank account in Traven's name in Acapulco. When John Huston filmed *The Treasure of the Sierra Madre* in 1947, a man claiming to be Traven's agent visited the set and appeared to take an unusual interest in the proceedings, but he disappeared afterward.

Apparently that's how he wanted it: It now appears that the writer took on at least four distinct identities during his lifetime. One of these men wrote, "I shall always and at all times prefer to be pissed on by dogs than reveal who I am."

• • •

KEEPSAKE

In 1881, as the nation was mourning James Garfield's assassination, the following advertisement appeared in 200 newspapers:

❝ I have secured the authorized steel engravings of the late President Garfield, executed by the United States Government, approved by the President of the United States, by Congress and by every member of the President's family as the most faithful of all portraits of the President. It was executed by the Government's most expert steel engravers, and I will send a copy from the original plate, in full colors approved by the Government, postpaid, for one dollar each.

Each reader who sent in a dollar received the promised engraving—on a 5¢ postage stamp.

• • •

GOOD ENOUGH

Ixonia, Wisconsin, was named at random.

Unable to agree on a name for the town, the residents printed the alphabet on slips of paper, and a girl named Mary Piper drew letters successively until a name was formed.

The town was christened Ixonia on Jan. 21, 1846, and it remains the only Ixonia in the United States.

• • •

SUBTEXT

John Brunner's 1965 science fiction novel *The Squares of the City* concerns a South American metropolis in which two opposing political leaders direct the actions of their followers using "subliminal perception."

In an afterword, Brunner revealed that he had organized the entire plot to follow a historic chess game, Steinitz-Tchigorin Havana 1892. Each of the 32 pieces and pawns corresponds to a character in the book, and every capture in the Steinitz-Tchigorin game corresponds to an event in the plot. For example, Felipe Mendoza, representing the black king's bishop, is killed in a duel with Luis Arrio, who represents the white queen's knight. In the game, Steinitz captured Tchigorin's king's bishop with his queen's knight on move 22.

"The individuals who correspond to the 'pieces' have powers roughly commensurate with those of the pawns and officers they represent," Brunner explained. "The moves are all there, in their correct order and—so far as possible—in precise correspondence with their effect on the original game. That is to say, support of one piece by another on its own side, threatening of one or more pieces by a piece on the other side, indirect threats and the actual taking of pieces, are all as closely represented as possible in the development of the action."

The book was nominated for the Hugo Award for best novel in 1966.

• • •

CAST AWAY

Here's a paragraph from *Robinson Crusoe*. It contains a remarkable error—can you spot it?

❝A little after noon, I found the sea very calm, and the tide ebbed so far out, that I could come within a quarter of a mile of the ship; and here I found a fresh renewing of my grief: for I saw evidently, that if we had kept on board, we had been all safe—that is to say, we had all got safe on shore, and I had not been so miserable as to be left entirely destitute of all comfort and company, as I now was. This forced tears from my eyes again; but as there was little relief in that, I resolved, if possible, to get to the ship—so I pulled off my clothes, for the weather was hot to extremity, and took the water. But when I came to the ship, my difficulty was still greater to know how to get on board; for, as she lay aground and high out of the water, there was nothing within my reach to lay hold of. I swam round her twice, and the second time I spied a small piece of rope, which I wondered I did not see at first, hang down by the fore-chains, so low as that with great difficulty I got hold of it, and, by the help of that rope, got up into the forecastle of the ship. Here I found that the ship was bulged, and had a great deal of water in her hold, but that she lay so on the side of a bank of hard sand, or rather earth, and her stern lay lifted up upon the bank, and her head low almost to the water: by this means all her quarter was free, and all that was in that part was dry; for you may be sure my first work was to search and to see what was spoiled, and what was free, and first I found that all the ship's provisions were dry and untouched by the water: and being very well disposed to eat, I went to the bread-room and filled my pockets with biscuit, and ate it as I went about other things, for I had no time to lose. I also found some rum in the great cabin, of which I took a large dram, and which I had indeed need enough of to spirit me for what was before me. Now I wanted nothing but a boat, to furnish myself with many things which I foresaw would be very necessary to me.

• • •

TALL AND WIDE

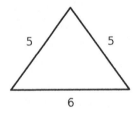 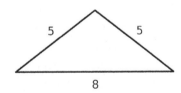

Which of these triangles has the greater area?

(See Answers and Solutions)

• • •

MOST WANTED

In 2007 Irish police noticed an alarming trend: They had written more than 50 tickets to one driver, a Prawo Jazdy. In traffic stops he had offered Polish credentials with varying addresses, and the repeated citations had failed to improve his driving. In June they realized their mistake: Prawo Jazdy is Polish for "driver's license."

• • •

PAN KING

Excerpts from the reviews of James William Davison, music editor of the London *Times* from 1846 to 1878:

* "Perhaps a more overrated man never existed than this same Schubert."
* "[Schumann is] the very opposite of good."
* "We should rather be inclined to class [Berlioz] a daring lunatic than as a sound, healthy musician."
* "Never was a writer of operas so destitute of real invention, so destitute in power or so wanting in the musician's skill [as Verdi]."
* "The entire works of Chopin present a motley surface of ranting hyperbole and excruciating cacophony."
* "[Wagner] is such queer stuff that criticism would be thrown away upon it."
* "He who imagines that, at any time within the last half century Franz Liszt was a musical composer must entertain either very odd notions of art or must be, *qua* music, an absolute ignoramus."

But: "[William Sterndale Bennett] lives with us in his works. The music he created conquered, in some sense, the power of death."

PART EIGHT

MOTHER'S DAY, EAGLES, *and* HARRY HOUDINI

FAIR ENOUGH

Apocryphal but entertaining: During one of Norbert Wiener's talks on cybernetics, a student raised an esoteric point.

Wiener said, "Why, that's as improbable as a bunch of monkeys having typed out the *Encyclopaedia Britannica*."

The student said brightly, "But that's happened once, anyway."

• • •

BREAKING IN

Gelett Burgess published his first poem through a "literary burglary." On noticing that most of the "notes and queries" in the *Boston Transcript* were inquiries about obscure poems, he submitted this letter:

Dear Editor

Who is the author of the poem commencing 'The dismal day with dreary pace,' and can you give me the verses?

F.E.C.

Then he submitted a response:

Editor of the 'Transcript':

The author of the poem commencing 'The dreary day' etc., is Frank Gelett Burgess, and the whole poem is as follows:

The dismal day with dreary pace
Hath dragged its tortuous length along;
The gravestones black, and funeral vase
Cast horrid shadows long.

Oh, let me die, and never think
Upon the joys of long ago;
For cankering thoughts make all the world
A wilderness of woe.

J.V.Z.

"Of course it was printed," he wrote later. "You see it's easy when you know how."

• • •

DOUBLE DREAD

Lyssophobia is fear of hydrophobia.

• • •

THE PIGGY BANK

You have 100 coins totaling $5.00. They consist of pennies, dimes, and half dollars. How many of each are there?

(See Answers and Solutions)

• • •

SHORTHAND

University of Michigan mathematician Norman Anning offered this "non-commutative soliloquy of an introspective epistemologist" in *Scripta Mathematica* in 1948:

[(N + H)ow + (T + W)hat](I know).

Expand the expression and you get *Now I know how I know that I know what I know.*

• • •

STICK FIGHT

The Rod of Asclepius, left, with a single snake, is the symbol of medicine. Unfortunately, a large number of commercial American medical organizations instead use the caduceus, right, which has two snakes. Asclepius was the Greek god of healing, but the caduceus was wielded by Hermes and connotes commerce, negotiation, and trickery.

The confusion began when the American military began using the caduceus in the late 19th century, and it persists today. In a survey of 242 healthcare logos (reported in his 1992 book *The Golden Wand of Medicine*), Walter Friedlander found that 62 percent of professional associations used the rod of Asclepius, while 76 percent of commercial organizations used the caduceus.

"If it's got wings on it, it's not really the symbol of medicine," the communications director of the Minnesota Medical Association told author Robert Taylor. "Some may find it hard to believe, but it's true. It's something like using the logo for the National Rifle Association when referring to the Audubon Society."

• • •

TRIBUTE

Japanese novelist Taro Hirai wrote detective fiction under the pseudonym Edogawa Ranpo.

That's a phonetic rendering of one of the genre's inventors— Edgar Allan Poe.

• • •

FOLLOWING ORDERS

66 A Roman Catholic who had filled up the measure of his iniquities as far as he dared went to the priest to confess and obtain absolution. He entered the apartment of the priest and addressed him thus, 'Holy father, I have sinned.'

The priest bade him kneel before the penitential chair. The penitent was looking about, and saw the priest's gold watch lying upon the table within his reach; he seized it and put it in his bosom. The priest approached him and requested him to acknowledge the sins for which he wished absolution.

'Father,' said the rogue, 'I have stolen, and what shall I do?' 'Restore,' said the priest, 'the thing you have stolen to its rightful owner.' 'Do you take it,' said the penitent. 'No, I shall not,' said the priest; 'you must give it to the owner.' 'But he has refused to take it.' 'If this be the case you may keep it.'

The priest granted him full absolution; and the penitent knelt and kissed his hand, craved his benediction, crossed himself, and departed with a clear conscience, and a very valuable gold watch into the bargain.

—Walter Baxendale, *Dictionary of Anecdote,*
Incident, Illustrative Fact, 1888

• • •

ENOUGH

On Nov. 20, 1820, the Nantucket whaler *Essex* was attacking a pod of sperm whales in the South Pacific when an immense 85-foot whale surfaced about 100 yards off the bow. It spouted two or three times, dove briefly, then charged and "struck the ship with his head just forward of the fore chains," reported mate Owen Chase. "He gave us such an appalling and tremendous jar as nearly threw us all on our faces. The ship brought up as suddenly and violently as if she had struck a rock, and trembled for a few moments like a leaf. We looked at each other in perfect amazement, deprived almost of the power of speech."

The whale passed under the ship and lay on the surface, stunned at first and then convulsing. Chase ordered men to the pumps and called back the boats, but as the *Essex* began to settle in the water a man called, "Here he is—he is making for us again."

"I turned around, and saw him about one hundred rods directly ahead of us, coming down with apparently twice his ordinary speed, and to me it appeared with tenfold fury and vengeance in his aspect," Chase wrote. "The surf flew in all directions, and his course towards us was marked by a white foam of a rod in width, which he made with a continual violent threshing of his tail." The second blow stove in the *Essex*'s bows, and the whale "passed under the ship again, went off to leeward, and we saw no more of him."

If this was vengeance, it was well accomplished. The *Essex* sank more than 1,000 miles from land; of the 21 crew who piled into three boats, only eight would survive, three on a barely habitable island and five after resorting to cannibalism during three months at sea. The whale acquired a further kind of immortality: Chase's account of the disaster, written on his return to Massachusetts, helped inspire Herman Melville to write *Moby-Dick*.

• • •

IN A WORD

accubation
n. the act or posture of reclining on a couch

pogonotrophy
n. the growing of a beard

ultracrepidate
v. to criticize beyond sphere of one's knowledge

dolorifuge
n. anything that drives away pain

• • •

UNITED NATIONS

"England's not a bad country—it's just a mean, cold, ugly, divided, tired, clapped-out, post-imperial, post-industrial slag heap covered in polystyrene hamburger cartons."—Margaret Drabble

"Belgium is a country invented by the British to annoy the French."—Charles de Gaulle

"In India, 'cold weather' is merely a conventional phrase and has come into use through the necessity of having some way to distinguish between weather which will melt a brass doorknob and weather which only makes it mushy."—Mark Twain

"The Americans . . . have invented so wide a range of pithy and hackneyed phrases that they can carry on an amusing and animated conversation without giving a moment's reflection to what they are saying and so leave their minds free to consider the more important matters of big business and fornication."—Somerset Maugham

"In any world menu, Canada must be considered the vichyssoise of nations—it's cold, half-French, and difficult to stir."—Stuart Keate

• • •

A FAVOR

Lend me $10, but give me only half of it.
Then you'll owe me $5, and I'll owe you $5, and we'll be even.

• • •

MISSION ACCOMPLISHED

In 356 B.C., Herostratus set fire to the Temple of Artemis.
He said he did it to immortalize his name.
He succeeded.

• • •

ONE SOLUTION

Excerpt from the 1791 will of an English gentleman who had
been sent unwillingly to live in Tipperary:

66 I give and bequeath the annual sum of ten pounds, to
be paid in perpetuity out of my estate, to the following purpose. It is my will and pleasure that this sum shall be spent
in the purchase of a certain quantity of the liquor vulgarly
called whisky, and it shall be publicly given out that a certain number of persons, Irish only, not to exceed twenty, who
may choose to assemble in the cemetery in which I shall be
interred, on the anniversary of my death, shall have the same
distributed to them. Further, it is my desire that each shall
receive it by half-a-pint at a time till the whole is consumed,
each being likewise provided with a stout oaken stick and a
knife, and that they shall drink it all on the spot. Knowing
what I know of the Irish character, my conviction is, that
with these materials given, they will not fail to destroy each
other, and when in the course of time the race comes to be
exterminated, this neighbourhood at least may, perhaps, be
colonized by civilized and respectable Englishmen.

— Virgil McClure Harris, *Ancient, Curious*
and Famous Wills, 1911

• • •

CONNECTION

At 3:35 a.m. on Aug. 14, 1888, off the coast of Nova Scotia, Second Officer Jørgensen of the Danish steamer *Geiser* was asleep in his bunk when he was awakened by a "frightful crash." As he rolled out of his bunk, the bow of another ship "crashed its way through the walls of my stateroom, making an enormous hole and blocking the door so I couldn't get out." Desperately he grabbed the anchor chain of the strange ship "and climbed up to her deck just as the *Geiser* gave one last lurch and went down out of sight, with her decks covered with shrieking, despairing people."

He found himself aboard *Geiser*'s sister ship *Thingvalla*, which had been plying the same line between New York and Copenhagen. In the stormy night, *Thingvalla*'s prow had struck *Geiser* amidships, and she sank in seven minutes. *Thingvalla*'s boats rescued 14 passenger and 17 crew, leaving 126 unaccounted for—most of the passengers died in their bunks.

• • •

SANCTUARY

Oxfordshire's annual stag hunt took a strange turn in 1819:

66 Dec. 21, being St. Thomas's Day, as usual, a stag was turned out from Blenheim Park, the property of his Grace, the Duke of Marlborough. It directed its course towards Wickham; from thence it took the high road and proceeded to Oxford; and then formed one of the most beautiful and picturesque sights that can be imagined. The stag, and dogs

in close pursuit, followed by a great number of well-known and experienced sportsmen, proceeded up the High-street, as far as Brazenose College; when, to the no small astonishment of hundreds of spectators, the stag took refuge in the chapel, during divine service; where it was killed, *sans ceremonie*, by the eager dogs.

From *The Gentleman's Magazine*, January 1820.

• • •

SPANAGRAMS

Arithmetic is easy in Spanish—just rearrange letters:

UNO + CATORCE = CUATRO + ONCE
DOS + TRECE = TRES + DOCE
DOCE + TRES = TRECE + DOS

• • •

THE TWO CULTURES

In 1855 American publisher James T. Fields made the mistake of taking William Thackeray to a dull scientific lecture:

❝ During his second visit to Boston I was asked to invite him to attend an evening meeting of a scientific club, which was to be held at the house of a distinguished member. I was very reluctant to ask him to be present, for I knew he could be easily bored, and I was fearful that a prosy essay or geological speech might ensue, and I knew he would be exasperated with me, even although I were the innocent cause of his affliction. My worst fears were realized. We had hardly got seated, before a dull, bilious-looking old gentleman rose, and applied his auger with such pertinacity that we were all bored nearly to distraction. I dared not look at Thackeray, but I felt that his eye was upon me. My distress may be imagined, when he got up quite deliberately from the prominent place where a chair had been set for him, and made his exit very noiselessly into a small anteroom leading into the larger room, and in which no one was sitting. The small apartment was dimly lighted, but he knew that I knew he was there. Then commenced a series of pantomimic feats impossible to describe adequately. He threw an imaginary person (myself, of course) upon the floor, and proceeded to stab him several times with a paper-folder which he caught up for the purpose. After disposing of his victim in this way, he was not satisfied, for the dull lecture still went on in the other room, and he fired an imaginary revolver several times at an imaginary head. Still, the droning speaker proceeded with his frozen subject (it was something about the Arctic regions, if I remember rightly), and now began the greatest pantomimic scene of all, namely, murder by poison, after the manner in which the player King is disposed of in Hamlet. Thackeray had found a small phial on the mantel-shelf, and out of it he proceeded to pour the imaginary 'juice of cursed hebenon' into the imaginary porches of somebody's ears. The whole thing was inimitably done, and I hoped nobody saw it but myself; but years afterwards a ponderous, fat-witted young man put the question squarely to me: 'What was the matter with Mr. Thackeray that night the club met at M——'s house?'

• • •

TOO MUCH GLORY

When Louis XIV asked, "What time is it?", he was told, "Whatever time your majesty desires."

When Louis comforted the duke of Saint-Aignan on the death of his son, Roger de Rabutin wrote, "It is only near him that a parent can find some pleasure in losing his children."

When Louis asked Boileau's opinion of his verses, the poet said, "Ah, sire, I am convinced that nothing is impossible to your majesty. You desired to write some poor rhymes, and you have succeeded in making them positively detestable."

During a lecture on chemistry, Louis Jacques Thénard told Charles X, "These gases are going to have the honor of combining before your majesty."

The subjects of James I expressed the wish that he might reign over them as long as the sun, moon, and stars should endure. "I suppose, then," muttered the king, "they mean my successor to reign by candlelight."

• • •

ADVENTURES IN TUITION

In 1987, University of Illinois freshman Mike Hayes wrote to *Chicago Tribune* columnist Bob Greene with a modest proposal: that each of Greene's readers contribute a penny to finance his education.

"Just one penny," he told Greene. "A penny doesn't mean anything to anyone. If everyone who is reading your column looks around the room right now, there will be a penny under the couch cushion, or on the corner of the desk, or on the floor. That's all I'm asking. A penny from each of your readers."

Greene published the appeal in 200 newspapers via his syndicated column—and Hayes received 77,000 letters and enough pennies to break his bank's coin-counting machine three times. He easily reached his goal of $28,000, enough for four years of tuition, room and board, and books.

He graduated with a degree in food science. Asked why the scheme worked, he said, "I didn't ask for a lot of money. I just asked for money from a lot of people."

• • •

SKY CHARIOT

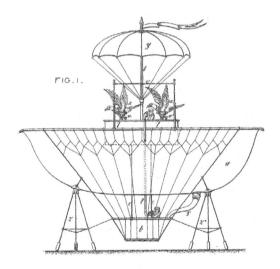

FIG. I.

Balloons are nifty, but they're hard to steer, and conventional motor-driven propellers are too heavy. So in 1887, Frenchman Charles Wulff proposed tying eagles to the car to form living propellers.

The birds would wear shoulder straps to keep them in place. The man in the car shouts his destination into a speaking tube, and the conductor uses a hand wheel and rollers to point the birds in the appropriate direction "quite independently of their own will." A net can be lowered to stop them from flapping.

What could go wrong?

• • •

NO MESSAGE

When he wasn't escaping straitjackets, Harry Houdini spent a lot of time debunking spiritualists.

Shortly before his death, he made a pact with his wife, Bess: If possible, he would contact her from the other side and deliver a prearranged coded message.

When he died, Bess lit a candle beside his photograph and kept it burning for 10 years, holding séances every Halloween to test the pact. Harry never spoke.

In 1936, after a final attempt on the roof of the Knickerbocker Hotel, Bess put out the candle.

"Ten years is long enough to wait for any man," she said.

• • •

HINTIKKA'S PARADOX

(1) If a thing can't be done without something wrong being done, then the thing itself is wrong.

(2) If X is impossible and Y is wrong, then I can't do both X and Y, and I can't do X but not Y.

But if Y is wrong and doing X-but-not-Y is impossible, then by (1) it's wrong to do X.

Hence if it's impossible to do a thing, then it's wrong to do it.

• • •

LINCOLN SEEKS EQUALITY

You're in a pitch-dark room. On a table before you are 12 pennies. You know that 5 are heads up and 7 are tails up, but you don't know which are which. By moving and flipping the coins you must produce two piles with an equal number of heads in each pile. How can you do this without seeing the coins?

(See Answers and Solutions)

• • •

MISC

- No bishop appears in *Through the Looking-Glass.*
- Can a law compel us to obey the law?
- $98415 = 9^{8-4} \times 15$
- Why does the ghost haunt Hamlet rather than Claudius?
- "Put me down as an anti-climb Max."—Max Beerbohm, declining to hike to the top of a Swiss Alp

• • •

UNQUOTE

"You develop an instant global consciousness, a people orientation, an intense dissatisfaction with the state of the world, and a compulsion to do something about it. From out there on the moon, international politics look so petty. You want to grab a politician by the scruff of the neck and drag him a quarter of a million miles out and say, 'Look at that, you son of a bitch.'"

—Apollo 14 astronaut Edgar Mitchell

• • •

THE PARENT TRAP

The founder of Mother's Day, Anna Jarvis, had no children of her own and decried the commercialization of the holiday.

Jarvis had proposed a national Mother's Day in 1907, in part to honor her own mother. She promoted the idea with governors, congressmen, editors, and the White House, and in 1914 Woodrow Wilson set aside the second Sunday in May to honor the nation's mothers. But the holiday was almost immediately co-opted by merchants, a turn that horrified Jarvis. "Confectioners put a white ribbon on a box of candy and advance the price just because it's Mother's Day," she complained in 1924. "There is no connection between candy and this day. It is pure commercialization."

She tried to stem the tide by legal means, incorporating herself as the Mother's Day International Association and threatening copyright suits against what she felt were commercial celebrations. She had recommended the wearing of carnations to mark the holiday; when florists raised the price she distributed celluloid buttons instead at her own expense.

She reserved a special bitterness for sons who bought mass-produced cards for their mothers. "A maudlin, insincere printed card or ready-made telegram means nothing except that you're too lazy to write to the woman who has done more for you than anyone else in the world," she said. "Any mother would rather have a line of the worst scribble from her son or daughter than any fancy greeting card."

"The sending of a wire is not sufficient. Write a letter to your mother. No person is too busy to do this."

It was hopeless. Her spirit never flagged, but her finances began to give way, and in 1943, penniless and almost blind, she was admitted to a Philadelphia hospital. Her friends pledged funds for her support, but she died in a West Chester sanitarium in 1948.

• • •

TURNABOUT

In 1870 the Duke of Wellington received a letter from Sir Charles Russell. He was restoring a certain church and had taken the liberty of putting Wellington's name down for a donation.

"Dear Sir Charles," Wellington replied, "I too am restoring a church, and if we both agree to give the same amount, no money need pass between us. Yours, Wellington."

• • •

ART DIRECTION

In 1879, illustrator Emily Gertrude Thomson appointed to meet Lewis Carroll at the South Kensington Museum. She had arrived at the rendezvous before she realized that neither of them knew what the other looked like.

"The room was fairly full of all sorts and conditions, as usual," she wrote later, "and I glanced at each masculine figure in turn, only to reject it as a possibility of the one I sought."

As the clock struck, she heard high voices and children's laughter ringing down the corridor, and a tall, slim gentleman entered holding two little girls by the hand. "He stood for a moment, head erect, glancing swiftly over the room, then, bending down, whispered something to one of the children; she, after a moment's pause, pointed straight at me."

He dropped their hands, came forward with a smile, and said, "I am Mr. Dodgson; I was to meet you, I think?" She smiled and asked how he had recognized her.

"My little friend found you," he said. "I told her I had come to meet a young lady who knew fairies, and she fixed on you at once."

• • •

STREET MARKETING

Physicists Chen Ning Yang and Tsung-Dao Lee used to discuss their work over lunch at a Chinese restaurant on 125th Street in Manhattan. One day they made an important insight into parity violation, and the two received the 1957 Nobel Prize in physics. After the award was announced, one of them noticed a sign in the restaurant window: "Eat here, get Nobel Prize."

• • •

COMMAND PERFORMANCE

The Bavarian village of Oberammergau has a special deal with God. While the bubonic plague was ravaging Europe, the town's citizens vowed that if they were spared they would perform a play every 10 years depicting the life and death of Jesus.

God, apparently, accepted. The death rate among adults rose from 1 in October 1632 to 20 in March 1633, but then it dropped again to 1 in July 1633.

True to their word, the villagers staged a play in 1634, and they've done so every 10 years ever since.

• • •

BURYING THE HATCHET

The Third Punic War didn't end until 1985.

Begun in 149 B.C., the contest never reached a peace treaty because Rome utterly destroyed Carthage. 2,134 years passed before the cities' mayors "officially" ended the conflict.

• • •

SEE ALSO

"The Passionate *Encyclopedia Britannica* Reader to His Love":

As And to Aus, and Aus to Bis;
As Hus to Ita, and Ita to Kys;
As Pay to Pol, and Pol to Ree;
Ah, that is how you are to me!

As Bis to Cal, and Cal to Cha;
As Edw to Eva, and Eva to Fra;
As Ref to Sai, and Sai to Shu;
That is, I hope, how I'm to you.

—*New York Tribune*, quoted in *Life*, April 14, 1921

• • •

THE TIES THAT BIND

The Spanish word *esposa* means both "wife" and "handcuff."

• • •

THE EASY WAY

Ludwig Schlekat bought a bank with its own money. Over the

course of 17 years, starting in 1936, he embezzled $600,000 from the Parnassus National Bank of New Kensington, Pa. Then he invented two fictional investors and arranged for them to buy the bank and make him president.

In his new position he earned $800 a month, four times the salary he'd been getting as a teller. He bought a $19,500 home, $13,000 in furnishings, and a $1,000 diamond for his wife. When regulators pounced on these he resisted, saying they'd been bought with earned rather than stolen money. He went to jail for 10 years.

• • •

CAMEO

The last canto of Dante's *Purgatorio* contains this perplexing sentence:

And if perchance
My saying, dark as Themis or as Sphinx,
Fail to persuade thee, (since like them it foils
The intellect with blindness) yet ere long
Events shall be the Naiads, that will solve
This knotty riddle, and no damage light
On flock or field.

When did water nymphs solve the riddle of the Sphinx? It turns out that Dante was relying on a flawed medieval edition of Ovid's *Metamorphoses* that rendered *Laïades* (meaning Oedipus, the son of Laius) as *Naïades*, or naiads. He believed that water nymphs had ridden their sea monsters across the desert to solve the Sphinx's riddle.

The version of the story that we know, in which Oedipus

solves the riddle, comes from Sophocles' *Oedipus*, which, being written in Greek, was unavailable to Dante. And he cast his own version in such exquisite language that it's now immortal—one classic work misquoting another.

• • •

LEAP DAY

Alice gets a rocket-powered pogo stick for her birthday. She jumps 1 foot on the first hop, 2 feet on the second, then 4, 8, and so on. This gets alarming. By judicious hopping, can she arrange to return to her starting point?

(See Answers and Solutions)

• • •

EXEUNT

Unusual methods adopted by suicide victims, compiled by George Kennan for a report in *McClure's Magazine*, 1908:

- Hanging themselves, or taking poison, in the tops of high trees
- Throwing themselves upon swiftly revolving circular saws
- Exploding dynamite in their mouths
- Thrusting red-hot pokers down their throats
- Hugging red-hot stoves
- Stripping themselves naked and allowing themselves to freeze to death on winter snowdrifts out of doors, or on piles of ice in refrigerator-cars
- Lacerating their throats on barbed-wire fences

- Drowning themselves head downward in barrels
- Suffocating themselves head downward in chimneys
- Diving into white-hot coke-ovens
- Throwing themselves into craters of volcanoes
- Shooting themselves with ingenious combinations of a rifle with a sewing-machine
- Strangling themselves with their hair
- Swallowing poisonous spiders
- Piercing their hearts with corkscrews and darning-needles
- Cutting their throats with handsaws and sheep-shears
- Hanging themselves with grape vines
- Swallowing strips of underclothing and buckles of suspenders
- Forcing teams of horses to tear their heads off
- Drowning themselves in vats of soft soap
- Plunging into retorts of molten glass
- Jumping into slaughter-house tanks of blood
- Decapitation with home-made guillotines
- Self-crucifixion

"One would naturally suppose that a person who had made up his mind to commit suicide would do so in the easiest, most convenient, and least painful way," Kennan concludes, "but the literature of the subject proves conclusively that hundreds of suicides, every year, take their lives in the most difficult, agonizing, and extraordinary ways; and that there is hardly a possible or conceivable method of self-destruction that has not been tried."

• • •

MAIL SNAIL

In December 1924, a postal inspector from Corinth, Miss., leveled a series of charges against the postmaster at the University of Mississippi. "You mistreat mail of all classes," he wrote, "including registered mail; . . . you have thrown mail with return postage guaranteed and all other classes into the garbage can by the side entrance," and "some patrons have gone to this garbage can to get their magazines."

The slothful postmaster was William Faulkner. He had accepted the position in 1921 while trying to establish himself as a writer, but he spent most of his time in the back of the office, as far as possible from the service windows, in what he called the "reading room." When he wasn't reading or writing there he was playing bridge with friends; he would rise grumpily only when a patron rapped on the glass with a coin.

It was a brief career. Shortly after the inspector's complaint, Faulkner wrote to the postmaster general: "As long as I live under the capitalistic system, I expect to have my life influenced by the demands of moneyed people. But I will be damned if I propose to be at the beck and call of every itinerant scoundrel who has two cents to invest in a postage stamp. This, sir, is my resignation."

ANSWERS *and* SOLUTIONS

BURNING TIME (PAGE 6)

Double one fuse and light both its ends. At the same time, light the second fuse. The first fuse will burn out in 30 minutes. When it does, light the remaining end of the second fuse. When that fuse burns out, 45 minutes will have passed.

• • •

COVERUP (PAGE 15)

No. Color the squares as shown. Now each tile must cover a black, a gray, and a white square. If we're to cover the figure completely, then it must contain an equal number of squares of each color. But it contains 19 black, 17 gray, and 18 white squares. So the task is impossible.

• • •

HAND COUNT (PAGE 23)

If no two people are to reach the same handshake total, then the most gregarious person in the stadium must shake 49,999 hands, the next-most-gregarious 49,998, and so on. But that means the shyest person would shake zero hands—which is impossible, since the gregarious person shook every hand in the place.

Alternatively, if the shyest person shakes one hand, then to avoid any duplication the gregarious person would have to shake 50,000 hands, which is also impossible, as there are only 49,999 hands available for him to shake. Therefore there must be at least two participants, somewhere, who have shaken the same number of hands.

• • •

BALL JUGGLING (PAGE 36)

Because the moon's shadow is smaller than Earth's, a total solar eclipse is visible only from within a relatively narrow latitude on Earth's surface, while a lunar eclipse is visible from anywhere on the night side of the planet. For the same reason, a total solar eclipse lasts for only a few minutes at any given location, while a lunar eclipse lasts for several hours.

• • •

EMPTIED NEST (PAGE 45)

Square both sides:

$$x + \sqrt{x + \sqrt{x + \sqrt{x \ldots}}} = 4$$

Now we can substitute the original equation, giving $x + 2 = 4$ and $x = 2$.

• • •

THEY GROW UP SO FAST (PAGE 49)

Timmy's birthday is December 31, and today is January 1.

• • •

SIDELINE (PAGE 63)

Alexander Graham Bell.

• • •

THE FIVE ROOMS (PAGE 69)

It's impossible. Three of the rooms have five wall segments, an odd number. A continuous line that starts outside such a room and crosses all five wall segments will be "trapped" inside the room, with no way to exit. We can start the line in one five-walled room and end it in another, but the third presents an insoluble problem.

• • •

THE LAST CENT (PAGE 79)

Consider what happens if you leave your opponent 5 pennies. At that point, no matter how many he removes, you can play so as to leave the final penny to him. Now, if leaving him 5 pennies is a worthy target, then by the same principle so is leaving him 9 pennies: No matter how he plays, he must now give you the opportunity to leave him with 5. And going one step further, aiming for 13 pennies will ensure that you can reach 9, then 5, and victory. So, on your first turn, take 2 pennies.

• • •

PILLOW PROBLEM (PAGE 88)

BETRAYAL.

• • •

STRIDE RIGHT (PAGE 93)

Never. After the mother's first four strides and the daughter's first six, they will again step together with the right foot, and the cycle repeats. Nowhere in that interval do they step together with the left foot.

• • •

OPPOSITES EXACT (PAGE 97)

Call two opposing points A and B, and suppose that the temperature at A is higher than B. So A-B is positive. Now rotate both points around the equator, maintaining their opposition. Their difference can't remain positive, because we know that when they've traded places it will be negative (the opposite of its initial value). Because temperature varies continuously, there must be some position in between where their difference is zero.

• • •

SPIN CONTROL (PAGE 112)

It's better not to spin it. Two of the six chambers are loaded, so my chance of surviving was 4/6. But you know that the hammer fell on an empty chamber. Of the four empty chambers, only one is followed by a loaded one. So if you simply pull the trigger, you have a 3/4 chance of surviving. That's better than 4/6, so you're better off not spinning the cylinder.

• • •

SWINE WAVE (PAGE 119)

6	8
0	10

Arrange the pigs as above. Now:

8 is closer to 10 than 6.
10 is closer to 10 than 8.
Nothing is closer to 10 than 10.
6 is closer to 10 than 0.

Simple enough!

• • •

THE HANDICAP (PAGE 129)

Alexander will win again. We know that Alexander covers 100 meters in the time it takes Zachary to cover 97. If Alexander starts 3 meters behind the starting line, then the two brothers will be neck and neck at the 97-meter mark, and Alexander will pull ahead.

• • •

ALPHABET BLOCKS (PAGE 137)

No, it's not possible. Imagine painting the large cube with a checkerboard pattern. As we move through the alphabet we'll change colors at each step; if we're to succeed there must be 13 red cubes and 13 black ones (omitting the center cube). But a large checkerboard cube contains 12 cubes of one color and 14 of the other. So it can't be done.

• • •

"STEALING THE BELL ROPES" (PAGE 143)

❝❝Call the two ropes A and B. First tie the ends of A and B securely together. Then climb A and cut off B, leaving sufficient to tie a loop. Hanging with your arm through this loop, cut off A as high as you can reach, pull the severed A through the loop until you come nearly to the knot joining B, and descend by the doubled rope. Then pull through the loop and you have secured the greatest possible length of both ropes.

"If any reader should attempt to make use of this information for criminal purposes we can only hope that he will accidentally let fall the rope A after he has cut it through!"

• • •

MAKING WAY (PAGE 157)

If he runs toward the train, he'll cover the remaining 3/7 of the trestle and meet the train at the far end. This means that if he runs away from the train, he'll have covered 3/7 of the trestle (with 1/7 to go) when the train reaches the far end. He'll then run the remaining 1/7 while the locomotive crosses all 7/7 and passes him. So the train is traveling at 7 times his speed, or 140 kph.

• • •

AN INVITATION (PAGE 164)

David Homer Bates, manager of the War Department Telegraph Office, explains: "By reading the above backward, observing the phonetics, and bearing in mind that flesh is the equivalent of meat, the real meaning is easily found":

❝ If I should be in a boat off Aquia Creek at dark tomorrow (Wednesday) evening, could you without inconvenience meet me and pass an hour or two with me?—A. Lincoln

"It cannot be said that this specimen exhibits specially clever work on the part of the War Department staff, nor is it likely that the Confederate operator, if he overheard its transmission, had much trouble in unraveling its meaning. As to this we can only conjecture." Burnside understood it, and the two met.

• • •

SPUD LOOPS (PAGE 172)

Think of the potatoes as ghosts, and penetrate one with the other. The intersection of their surfaces forms the loop.

• • •

TALL AND WIDE (PAGE 184)

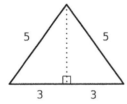 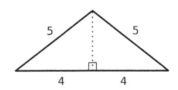

Each can be decomposed into two 3-4-5 triangles . . . so they're equal.

• • •

THE PIGGY BANK (PAGE 190)

Let P be the number of pennies, D the number of dimes, and H the number of half dollars.

$$P + D + H = 100$$

and

$$P + 10D + 50H = 500,$$

so

$$9D + 49H = 400.$$

Now, we know that H is less than 10, and the only value for which (400-49H) is divisible by 9 is 1. So the totals are 1 half dollar, 39 dimes, and 60 pennies.

"If you take care of your peonies," wrote Franklin P. Adams, "the dahlias will look after themselves."

• • •

LINCOLN SEEKS EQUALITY (PAGE 203)

Divide the pennies into two groups, one of 5 coins and one of 7. Then turn over all the coins in the smaller pile.

• • •

LEAP DAY (PAGE 210)

No. After n hops, Alice will have traveled at most $1 + 2 + 4 +\ldots + 2^{n-1} = 2^n-1$ feet from the starting point. But her very next hop will carry her $2n$ feet. So she must always overshoot the goal.

• • •

INDEX

last moments, bitterly reflective, 142
last sights, sobering, of western
  mice, 104
Latin, easily thrown around, 13
law
  and bootstraps, 203
  English, sort of just kidding
    around, 143
lawsuits, against oneself, 98
Lichtenberg, G.C., 89
life, difficulty of definition, 130
Lifeboat, Hitchcock cameo, 152
lighthouses, preferable to chapels, 115
limericks, 178
Lincoln, Abraham, might have
  mixed feelings about freedom of
  speech, 47
logic, demolished, 40, 49

Magellan, Ferdinand, and well-
  traveled slaves, 3
mail, useful as a history text, 59
Mailer, Norman, healthy self-
  regard, 166
man, a studious animal, 118
manslaughter by balloon, 43
Marshak, Samuil, surrounded by
  comedians, 47
Martians, communication with, 103
mathematics
  coincidental, 43
  cyclic numbers, 147
  with a meat cleaver, 155
mattresses, helium-filled, 40
Maugham, Somerset, 45
measurement, a relative matter,
  176
messages, otherworldly, copyright
  in, 167
Milne, A.A., non-bear recreations, 88
Mind, open to reason, 95

Moby-Dick, as journalism, 193
money
  acquisitive character of, 208
  poetically sought, 156
  and soul, not natural bedfellows, 86
Monopoly, and prison escapes, 96
monuments, French, unevenly
  distributed, 76
moon, paeans to, 105
Moorman, Scott, disappearance, 124
mother-daughter disagreements,
  mathematically unavoidable, 93
Mother's Day, a shameful travesty,
  204
Muir, John, and a wonderful dog, 11
murders
  of interrupted self-murderers,
    interrupted, 164
  midnight, 171
  pantomime, 198
  perfect, 127
music
  criticism, ill-considered, 185
  an impediment to war, 30

names
  assigned randomly, 182
  lawsuits, entertaining, 61
namesakes, victimized, 66
Nancy Drew, a counterfeit, 131
navies, humiliated, 72
Navy blimps, given to practical
  jokes, 118
Nelson, Horatio, memorably
  interred, 62
New York Times, wrong for 100
  years, 135
newspapers, commandeering
  Indians, 46
Ney, Michel, leaving with a bang,
  122

Made in United States
North Haven, CT
10 December 2021

12352589R00134